# COMBAT LEGEND

# FOCKE-WULF Fw 190

Peter Caygill

**Airlife**

First published in the UK in 2002
by Airlife Publishing Ltd

Text written by Peter Caygill
Profile illustrations drawn by Dave Windle
Cover painting by Jim Brown – The Art of Aviation Co. Ltd

**British Library Cataloguing-in-Publication Data**
A catalogue record for this book
is available from the British Library

ISBN 1 84037 366 0

Printed in China


For a complete list of all Airlife titles please contact:

**Airlife Publishing Ltd**
101 Longden Road, Shrewsbury, SY3 9EB, England
E-mail: sales@airlifebooks.com
Website: www.airlifebooks.com

# Contents

# Fw 190 Timeline

**1 June 1939**
First flight of Fw 190V-1 D-OPZE.

**7 August 1941**
6./JG 26, the first combat unit, begins to move its Fw 190A-1s from Le Bourget to Moorsele to begin operations over the Channel.

**29 August 1941**
*Leutnant* Heinz Schenk of 6./JG 26 becomes the first Fw 190 casualty when his A-1 (*Werke Nr 008*) is shot down by 'friendly fire' over Dunkirk after a dogfight with Spitfires.

**14 March 1942**
III./JG 2, led by *Hauptmann* Hans 'Assi' Hahn, becomes operational on the Fw 190A-1.

**23 June 1942**
*Oberleutnant* Armin Faber of 7./JG 2 presents his Fw 190A-3 to the RAF at Pembrey, allowing the British to make an assessment of the new German fighter.

**10 July 1942**
The first Fw 190A-3/U3 fighter-bombers of 10(*Jabo*)/JG 26 arrive at Caen-Carpiquet to prepare for operations along the south coast and against shipping in the English Channel.

**6 September 1942**
The first Fw 190A-3s arrive on the Eastern Front for I./JG 51.

**18 November 1942**
The first Fw 190s to reach the Mediterranean area are those of II./JG 2 transferred from north-western France.

**20 January 1943**
Fw 190A-4s of 10(*Jabo*)/JG 2 and 10(*Jabo*)/JG 26 carry out the largest daylight bombing attack on London since the Battle of Britain and the night Blitz.

**17/18 August 1943**
First major operation by the Fw 190A-5/U2s night-fighters of II./JG 300 during the RAF Bomber Command attack on Peenemunde.

**14 October 1943**
*Major* Walter Nowotny of I./JG 54 scores his 250th kill.

**11 January 1944**
First victory for *Sturmstaffel* 1, a B-17 shot down by *Oberleutnant* Othmar Zehart.

**13 January 1944**
*Leutnant* Emil Lang of II./JG 54 appears on the front cover of *Illustrierte Zeitung* magazine having set a record by shooting down eighteen aircraft in one day.

**23 January 1944**
The two-seat Fw 190A-8/U1 flies for the first time.

**7 July 1944**
The Fw 190A-8/R7 *Sturmbocks* of IV(*Sturm*)/JG 3 shoot down 23 Eighth Air Force bombers for the loss of two.

**15 August 1944**
III./JG 54 are withdrawn from France to be the first unit to re-equip with the Fw 190D-9.

**2 March 1945**
The *Stabsschwarm* of JG 301 receives the first Ta 152H-1 fighters.

# 1. Focke-Wulf Fw 190: Prototypes and Development

For those pilots of RAF Fighter Command who first encountered the Focke-Wulf Fw 190A in the late summer of 1941, there could be little doubt that the *Luftwaffe* had taken delivery of something special. They had been having a difficult enough time with the Messerschmitt Bf 109F, but the performance of the newcomer clearly put it in a different league. They would have been comforted to know that the new aircraft was still only in service in small numbers, and was beset by development problems. However, early suggestions that the new radial-engined fighters were ex-French Air Force Curtiss Hawk 75As that had been pressed into service would soon be seen as a rather poor joke. In fact the RAF knew a little about the new fighter, even at squadron level. Following a combat on 21 October 1941 between Spitfires of 72 Squadron and four aircraft with 'radial engines and square tipped wings' the squadron Operations Record Book commented: 'Several pilots reported the amazing speed and climb of the radial-engined aircraft – no doubt Fw 190s'.

The origins of the Fw 190 dated back to the autumn of 1937, when the *Reichsluftfahrt-ministerium* (RLM) placed a development contract with Focke-Wulf Flugzeugbau GmbH for a new single-engined interceptor. However, its genesis was to be far from straightforward. Some within the RLM, possibly influenced by Willi Messerschmitt and his supporters, could see no need for another single-seat fighter. Others, however, thought it highly desirable to obtain, as they put it, 'another iron in the fire'.

The choice of Focke-Wulf raised a few eyebrows. The company's previous single-seat fighter design, the parasol-winged Fw 159, had been less than successful in competition with the Messerschmitt Bf 109. However the quality of the Focke-Wulf design team, under the supervision of Dipl Ing Kurt Tank, was generally recognised. Work got under way in the spring of 1938, initially at a fairly leisurely pace, but by the summer officials at the RLM were applying severe pressure that would ultimately see the collapse of Rudi Blaser, Tank's head of design, from exhaustion.

## Ease of manufacture

As the forerunner of the second generation of single-engined monoplane fighters, the design philosophy of the Fw 190 was significantly different from that which had gone before. In marked contrast to R.J. Mitchell's Supermarine Spitfire, Tank and his team proposed a machine that offered ease of manufacture. They succeeded to the extent that using semi-skilled labour, firms that had not previously worked on high performance aircraft could build many components quickly and easily. This ideology was also to manifest itself in ease of maintenance, with much thought being given to the work of the *Luftwaffe*'s ground technicians. Their job, after all, would be to keep the aircraft flying, often in the most difficult and trying circumstances. Once in service, mechanics would appreciate the aircraft's numerous hinged panels. These had been made commendably large to allow easy access to the engine and armament, and could be removed altogether if the need arose.

Tank was given the opportunity to examine the Bf 109 in detail. He also had feedback from pilots who had flown the type with the Condor Legion in Spain. As a result, Tank was determined that his new fighter would possess much greater structural strength than the Messerschmitt design, a decision which was founded on first-hand knowledge gained in the First World War where he had seen the conditions in which the machinery of war had to operate. In several instances the specified structural requirements were exceeded by a considerable margin, in particular the undercarriage. This was designed to withstand a sinking speed of 15 ft/sec, nearly doubling the strength factor originally envisaged for the prototype. Such far-sightedness paid dividends: the Fw 190's undercarriage did not need any major re-design throughout its life, even though weight was to increase appreciably with the use of heavier weaponry and additional protective armour.

The wide track undercarriage also greatly eased pilot workload during taxying, take-off and landing, and was to result in a much lower accident rate than that which affected the Bf 109 with its closely spaced landing gear. This was

to be particularly appreciated in Russia. There, the conditions of mud and slush found on primitive airfields meant that ground handling was more of a hazard than on grass or paved surfaces. Unusually, the main undercarriage was electrically operated, although the tailwheel, which was semi-recessed in flight, was raised and lowered by a mechanical system linked to the main gear. Small pins projected through the upper surface of the wing to indicate to the pilot that the undercarriage was locked down. When taxying, braking was achieved hydraulically by activating toe brakes mounted on the rudder pedals.

## Radial engine

Power for the new fighter was to come, not from an in-line liquid-cooled Daimler-Benz DB 601 like the Bf 109, but from a BMW 139 air-cooled radial of 1,550 hp, coupled to a metal three-blade constant speed VDM propeller. This was a choice that went against contemporary thinking, since most designers favoured the use of in-line engines for high speed aircraft. Tank's willingness to use a radial engine was, in part, due to experience gained in testing several Russian Polikarpov I-16 fighters captured during the Spanish Civil War. As far as the RLM was concerned, use of the BMW 139 eased

The first prototype, Fw 190V-1, is seen in natural finish during initial taxying trials at Bremen immediately prior to its first flight on 1 June 1939. Test pilot Hans Sander is in the cockpit.

The Fw 190V-1 around the time of its first flight. By this time it carried the civilian registration D-OPZE and had been painted. The colours used included RLM 71 (dark green) and RLM 70 (black green) on the upper surfaces with RLM 65 (light blue) underneath. The tail band was red with a white disc and black Swastika. The registration letters on the fuselage were painted in gloss black.

some of the production worries that would undoubtedly have arisen if the Fw 190 had required Daimler-Benz power.

BMW, or to give it its full title, Bayerische Motorenwerke GmbH, could trace its history back to July 1917 when the Rapp Engine Works near Munich was acquired by wealthy entrepreneur Camillo Castiglioni. Initial production was of a six-cylinder, liquid-cooled engine of similar design to the 180 hp Mercedes that powered the Albatros D.V. The company's first involvement with air-cooled engines occurred in 1928 when a licence was acquired to sell, and then build, Pratt & Whitney Wasp and Hornet nine-cylinder radial engines. Experience with these engines led to the highly successful BMW 132 that powered the Junkers Ju 52, Henschel Hs 126 and Focke-Wulf Fw 200 among others.

The BMW 139 chosen for the Fw 190 was in effect two 132s combined to form a two-row radial, with a fan to assist with cooling. The choice of the BMW 139 fitted in well with Tank's design aims, as the engine was significantly more powerful than any liquid-cooled engine then in production and it was

also likely to be more rugged in operation. In particular, its lack of vulnerable cooling systems meant that it would probably be able to withstand battle damage to a much greater degree than in-line engines.

## First flight

Under relentless pressure from the RLM, the first prototype – Fw 190V-1 D-OPZE – quickly took shape in the works at Bremen. It made its first flight on 1 June 1939, with Focke-Wulf's Chief Test Pilot, Hans Sander, at the controls. The diminutive fighter, almost frail-looking on its stalky undercarriage, gave little indication of its inherent strength or of the power that lay underneath its expertly contoured engine cowling. Like previous Focke-Wulf aircraft it was named after a bird and was called the *Wurger*, a type known in the English-speaking world as the Shrike or Butcher-bird.

A novel feature of the first two prototypes was a ducted spinner, but this was quickly discarded in favour of a conventional spinner and NACA cowl when the hoped for improvement in high speed drag was not realised. A particularly neat touch was a

A fine view of Fw 190V-1 D-OPZE on its approach to landing, showing to advantage the original ducted spinner. It was hoped that this arrangement would reduce drag, but the practical benefits were small and it was quickly discarded in favour of a conventional spinner. Of note are the small doors on the wheels, which also did little to reduce drag. They too were to be deleted during development.

retractable stirrup set low on the left-hand side of the fuselage, which, together with a spring-loaded step set into the fuselage side, the pilot used to gain access to the cockpit. Much thought was given to the layout of the cockpit, which benefited greatly from input by Hans Sander, who in addition to being a highly gifted pilot, was a qualified engineer. Under a large canopy which gave an unprecedented view to the rear, the instruments were neatly laid out in a centre panel, with radio switches, undercarriage and flap actuation buttons, electrical circuit breakers and the like arranged on two consoles along each side of the cockpit.

The pilot's seating position was semi-reclined, which proved to be an advantage when it came to combating the effects of 'g' during high speed manoeuvring. The stick-operated electric tail trimmer was particularly appreciated, as were the low static friction control circuits that operated via push/pull rods and cables. All control surfaces featured fixed trim tabs. These could only be moved on the ground, but once they had been adjusted correctly, out-of-trim forces due to power and attitude changes were not pronounced. This resulted in relatively low stick forces. Control harmony was excellent, and although the elevators were a little on the heavy side, this was more than made up for by the light and responsive ailerons, which allowed rolls to be performed faster than in any other fighter.

## Superb performance

From the very first flight it was obvious that the new Fw 190 was a better performer than any other fighter then in service. Speeds of 370 mph were soon achieved, and the aircraft's rate of roll, climb performance and acceleration in the dive were exceptional. However, the new fighter was not perfect – its characteristic of toasting the pilot's feet owing to the proximity of the engine to the cockpit firewall was not welcome, and equally unpleasant was its habit of trying to gas him owing to the ingress of exhaust fumes into the cockpit. A problem was also experienced with the undercarriage up-locks, but replacing the original mechanism with a modified bomb release shackle soon solved this. Difficulties with the emergency canopy release at speeds in excess of 270 mph were eventually overcome by fitting an explosive device – a 20-mm cartridge which impacted against a piston, forcing the canopy backwards to where the airflow was sufficient to allow it to jettison cleanly, thus enabling the pilot to bale out.

## More powerful engine

Even before the prototype's first flight, BMW was offering its new 801 engine, a 14-cylinder two-row radial. It bore little resemblance to the BMW 139, its design owing much to the expertise of Bramo (Brandenburg Motorenwerke) with which BMW had merged in 1938. Although at 2,667 lb it was 360 lb heavier, it developed 1,600 hp, with the prospect of more to come. The difficulties experienced with the earlier engine led to a switch to the new type from the third prototype onwards. The engine mount had a total of five attachment points, two on the firewall and three on the main spar. The engine itself was fed via two self-sealing fuel tanks housed in the lower front fuselage and accessed via a ventral hatch. The tanks held 51 and 64 gallons.

Like the earlier BMW radial, it featured a large cooling fan. This was of twelve-bladed cast magnesium design, and operated at three times propeller speed to direct cooling air to the cylinders via closely fitting baffles. Even with this large fan, overheating was to be the major

problem during initial testing. Engine temperatures soared to unacceptable levels on numerous occasions, resulting in many test flights ending prematurely. On at least one occasion the heat build up was so intense that the ammunition for the 7.62-mm MG 17 fuselage-mounted machine-guns – which were fitted to the second prototype and subsequent aircraft – began to explode.

One fortunate outcome of the powerplant change, which was particularly appreciated by the flight test team at Focke-Wulf, was that the extra weight of the BMW 801 required the cockpit to be moved aft to maintain the correct centre of gravity. The modification considerably reduced cockpit temperature.

The other major modification undertaken during development concerned the wing. The first two prototypes (V-1 and V-2) and the first nine pre-production V-5 aircraft (V-3 and V-4 were not completed) possessed a wing span of 31 ft 2 in, whereas subsequent V-5 machines featured a wing of 33 ft 10 in span and reduced taper. The short span aircraft were referred to as V-5k (*kleine* – small) and the extended wing machines as V-5g (*grosse* – large). Wing areas were 160.4 sq ft and 196.5 sq ft respectively. The main reason for the change was the increase in

The first prototype Fw 190 with the ducted spinner removed and a normal spinner in its place. It also carries military markings FO+LY in place of the civilian registration used during initial flight trials. This particular machine was to have a long career and was used by the manufacturers for development trials until 1943.

A snowy scene at the Focke-Wulf plant in Bremen in the winter of 1939/40. The first prototype, Fw 190V-1 FO+LY, is towed towards the flight line. Note the Fw 200 Condor in the background.

all-up weight caused by use of the heavier BMW 801 engine (together with associated structural changes to accommodate it), the larger wing restoring the aircraft's manoeuvrability and climb rate, albeit at the expense of a small reduction in top speed.

Another feature of the Fw 190 that took a long time to work as it should was an advanced electro-hydraulically operated device known as the *Kommandogerat*. This was an engine control system intended to ease pilot workload by automatically taking care of fuel flow, mixture, propeller pitch settings, and ignition timing. It was also designed to automatically maintain the correct supercharger gear for flight at varying heights. This caused Kurt Tank some embarrassment on one occasion as the additional power cut in as he was in the middle of a loop, pitching him into a spin from which he only just recovered. The system was

operated via the pilot's throttle, and there was also a cut-out switch whereby manual control of the propeller pitch could be set if a pilot so desired.

## Pressure from above

Various measures were tried to solve the Fw 190's numerous problems, but with the passing of time and the demands of the service, there came a time when the inevitable question was raised. Would the promising design ever make it as an operational fighter? Time was running out for Kurt Tank and his team, with *Reichsmarschall* Hermann Goering exhorting the factory to, 'turn out Fw 190s like hot cakes,' and demands by the *Luftwaffe* that the aircraft be in service by mid-1941 at the latest.

By early 1941, most Fw 190 test flying was being carried out at the *Erprobungstelle der Luftwaffe* at Rechlin. Pilots seconded from operational units joined resident test pilots there. In March 1941 a small unit known as *Erprobungsstaffel* (Operational Test Squadron) 190 was formed at Rechlin. It comprised some thirty mechanics and engineers under *Oberleutnant* Otto Behrens, *Staffelkapitän* of 6./JG 26, and *Oberleutnant* Karl Borris, technical officer of II./JG 26. The two officers were immediately impressed by their new mounts, as they were far superior to the Bf 109Es they had been used to. They were also able to fly the new Focke-Wulf in mock combat with captured examples of the Spitfire. Although the latter still had the upper hand as regards turn performance, in every other aspect the Fw 190 was superior. In particular, its higher top speed, better climb and diving performance allowed the Focke-Wulf to dictate the terms of combat at all times. Behrens and Borris both had technical backgrounds, and despite the seemingly never-ending problems caused by overheating engines, fuel and oil leaks and runaway propellers, their championing of the aircraft was vital when it came to the Fw 190 surviving attacks from its detractors at the RLM.

By the summer of 1941 the modification programme carried out at Rechlin had at last produced a fighter that could be considered for active service. Early in August, Otto Behrens' unit transferred some of the first Fw 190A-1 production aircraft to Le Bourget, where they were used to begin the conversion of II *Gruppe* of JG 26, the *Schlageter Geschwader*.

Even though many minor snags had been fixed, engine problems would be common for some time to come. These were caused in part by one of Germany's most serious deficiencies – a shortage of suitable high quality metals, which were needed to produce alloys that could withstand the strength and temperature requirements of high performance engines.

## Fire hazards

Despite the fact that engine service life was not what it should have been and fires were to remain a hazard for some time to come, these difficulties were seen as an acceptable hazard when the *Luftwaffe* realised that it now had an interceptor fighter that possessed superior performance to anything that the opposition

Fw 190V-5 straight off the production line. It carried the *Werke* number 0005 on the fin and again under the canopy. V-5 series aircraft were the first to be powered by the BMW 801 engine. Early machines retained the early small wing, and were known as V-5k. Later aircraft were fitted with revised wings of increased span (V-5g).

could field. The only reservation concerned the aircraft's armament which, in the initial A-1 variant, comprised just four 7.62-mm MG 17 machine-guns.

## Engine reliability problems

Although the pilots may have been happy enough, the situation among the technical trades was far less rosy. Engines were often only fit for the scrap heap after a few hours flying time. The most frequent problem was the lower cylinder of the second bank, which continually broke its connecting rod. By now III./JG 26 was converting to the Fw 190 and its technical officer, *Oberleutnant* Rolf Schroedter, dispatched several failed units to the *Gruppe's* repair shop at Albert. Examination of the remains led to the conclusion that a relatively simple re-routeing of part of the exhaust system would reduce the temperature affecting the bottom-most cylinder, which in practice went a long way to solving the 190's problems. Soon engine hours could be measured in three figures. *Oberleutnant* Karl Borris (who had recently transferred to 8./JG 26 as its *Staffelführer*) was the grateful recipient of a gold watch from BMW when the engine in his

aircraft reached the previously unheard of figure of 100 hours flying time.

Although the Fw 190A's performance in most respects was superior to any other fighter of the time, it was not the best at everything. The older Bf 109F could still outperform the new fighter at altitude. The rated altitude of the BMW 801 engine was 23,000 ft, but at heights in excess of 20,000 ft the Fw 190's performance began to deteriorate. In 1941/42 this handicap was not seen as serious, since the Fw 190 was rarely required to fight at high altitude. On the Russian front most combats took place at low to medium levels. The Fw 190F and G ground-attack variants had even less reason than the fighter to operate at altitude. Developments of the Fw 190A, they are discussed in Chapter 5.

Even in the west, incursions into occupied Europe by RAF Fighter Command were rarely carried out much above 25,000 ft – the Spitfire V also began to lose its effectiveness above this height. However, the deficiency in the Fw 190's performance at altitude became more apparent from mid-1942, following the RAF's introduction of the much-improved Spitfire IX. Powered by a two-stage, two-speed supercharged Rolls-Royce Merlin 61, the Mark

An early Fw 190V-5 with the small wing of 31 ft 3 in span and area of 160 sq ft. The larger wing as fitted to the V-5g had a span of 33 ft 10 in and an area of 196 sq ft. Although use of the bigger wing reduced top speed by a small amount, climb rate and manoeuvrability were improved.

A close-up view of a BMW 801D-2 engine shows the grouping of the exhaust piping. The exhaust from eight cylinders was ejected as shown (two groups of four each side) with the other six cylinders exhausting under the fuselage. Serious problems with engine overheating very nearly led to the Fw 190 being abandoned. Hotspots occurred in the engine, in particular in the two lower cylinders on the rear bank, and it was not until the exhaust system was re-routed by engineers at JG 26 that the problem was largely overcome.

IX was 5-7 mph faster than the Fw 190A at 25,000 ft, an advantage that became even more apparent as height was increased.

## High altitude threat

Of greater significance was the gradual build up of attacks by USAAF Eighth Air Force B-17 and B-24 bombers that operated at heights of 25,000 ft or more. The bombers were given limited escort by RAF Spitfires and USAAF P-47 Thunderbolts, but as both fighters were short on range it was not until the arrival of the P-51 Mustang in late 1943 that fighter escort could be provided during deep penetration raids on German industry.

Although advanced versions of the Fw 190 were eventually developed that had much better altitude performance, they were not produced quickly enough or in sufficient numbers to combat the Mustangs that grew more numerous day by day, a situation that was to have dire consequences for the *Luftwaffe* and Germany during the last year and a half of the war.

Attempts to redress the 190's difficulties at high altitude led to the development of the Fw 190B and C. Late in 1942, four Fw 190As (*Werke* Nrs 0046–49) were modified as prototypes of the B-series, the first featuring a BMW 801D-2 with GM-1 nitrous oxide boost and a pressurised cabin. Although the first prototype B-0 had an enlarged wing of 40 ft 4 in span, the other machines retained the standard wing and also carried armament of two engine-mounted MG 17s with MG 151/20s in the wing roots. Testing was carried out at Hannover-Langenhagen and Rechlin, but was beset by continual problems with the pressurisation, which resulted in numerous leaks and occasional explosive blow-outs of the cockpit glazing. Only one 'production' Fw 190B-1 was produced, a rebuild of A-series *Werke* Nr 811.

More advanced still was the projected Fw 190C, which was intended to produce high power at altitude by employing a Hirth turbo-blower. In place of the familiar BMW 801, the first two C-series machines were powered by Daimler-Benz DB 603A engines of 1,750 hp,

The 12-bladed cooling fan as fitted to a BMW 801D-2 engine. It was of cast magnesium design and operated at three times propeller speed to provide cooling air not only to the cylinders, but also for the oil cooler, which was annular in form and was located in the forward part of the cowling.

although the annular radiator that they employed resulted in a most unusual nose profile for an in-line engine. The turbo-blower was first fitted to the next machine in the development sequence (V-18, *Werke* Nr 0040) producing an Fw 190 of radically different appearance to anything that had gone before. The length was increased to 31 ft 1 in and because of the increased power transmitted via a four-blade VDM propeller, the vertical tail surfaces had to be made considerably larger than on standard aircraft and were of wooden construction. The turbo-blower was fed by a large ventral intake.

Only six fully modified examples of the Fw 190C powered by the Daimler-Benz DB 603G of 2,000 hp were built. As this engine lacked proper development, some were replaced by the earlier DB 603A. Despite the fact that the Hirth 9-2281 blower performed satisfactorily, it was found that the ducting was unable to withstand the high exhaust gas temperatures, and failures were experienced after as little as ten hours' running. Development was continued over the next six months but in that time there was only a modest improvement. Although the Fw 190C had a service ceiling of 40,000 ft and could attain 415 mph at 36,000 ft, the technical problems associated with the blower were too great and it too was abandoned.

## Long-nose 'Dora'

Another reason for the abandonment of the Fw 190B and C was the promise being shown by the Fw 190D-9. This was powered by the 1,750 hp Junkers Jumo 213A, a 12-cylinder inverted-Vee, liquid-cooled engine with three-stage supercharging. The designation D-9 was applied as it was intended that it should supersede the A-8 on the production lines. It also featured an annular radiator mounted in front of the engine, which led some early observers to believe that the D-9 was powered by a radial. Use of the Jumo 213A increased overall length to 33 ft 5 in, and as a result the 'Dora' became known as the 'long-nosed' 190.

Power could be boosted to 2,240 hp with MW-50 injection, resulting in a top speed of 426 mph at 21,326 ft. Even at 33,000 ft, the D-9 was still capable of achieving 397 mph. Performance of this nature went a long way to restore the 190's reputation with friend and foe alike, especially as it transformed the aircraft's capabilities at altitude. Early examples of the D-series carried a standard hood but this was soon replaced by a bulged canopy which had first appeared on late production Fw 190F-8s. Development work was carried out by just three prototypes (Fw 190 V-17/U1, V-53 and V-54) and in marked contrast with the proposed B and C series, high levels of performance were obtained with very few development snags.

## 'Dora' enters service

The D-9 entered service with III./JG 54, commanded by *Major* Robert 'Bazi' Weiss, in the autumn of 1944 but its coming was not welcomed by everyone. Although it was faster

Fw 190 *Werke* Nr 0036 was built as an A-0 but was modified to become the V-13, the first prototype of the projected C-series. It is seen here with a 1,750 hp Daimler-Benz DB 603A 12-cylinder liquid-cooled engine with annular radiator and chin-mounted intake for the oil cooler. The outer wing guns were deleted to leave two engine-mounted MG 17s and two MG 151/20s in the wing roots.

and was a better performer at altitude, it lacked agility compared with the A-series (particularly in terms of rate of roll) and with only a pair of MG 131 machine-guns mounted above the engine and two MG 151/20 cannon in the wings, it was relatively lightly armed. Despite initial scepticism however, most pilots quickly got to like the Dora and many were to rate it as the best 190 of the lot. Unfortunately it was a case of too little too late as the aerial armadas that were attacking the German heartland day after day had built up an unstoppable momentum.

In the remaining months of the war the speed of the D-9 would come as a nasty shock to many P-51 and Spitfire IX pilots. The increased power of the Jumo 213A allowed it to turn tightly without losing momentum, and it also possessed a superior rate of climb and better diving acceleration than the Fw 190A – which was still outclassing most Allied fighters in these respects. The time taken to climb to 20,000 ft was just over seven minutes and the D-9's service ceiling was 39,372 ft.

The final adaptation of the Fw 190 design did not carry the Fw prefix, as it took the first two initials of designer Kurt Tank's name and became the Ta 152. Despite the new designation there was no doubting that the Ta 152 was the 'ultimate' Fw 190. Its similarity with the D-9 was marked; indeed, all experimental aircraft were re-worked examples of the earlier machine. Its most notable feature was a re-designed high aspect ratio wing spanning 47 ft 4 in, with the wing area being increased by approximately 25 per cent to 250.7 sq ft.

## The Ultimate 190

Although it came to be regarded as the finest piston-engined fighter produced by Germany during the Second World War, the Ta 152 again came too late, the prototype (the twice-rebuilt Fw 190A-O V-18/U2) flying for the first time in early October 1944. It crashed within a few days, and was replaced by Fw 190 V-20, which was powered by a Jumo 213E but retained the standard wing. The first prototype to feature full Ta 152 equipment was V-29/U1, which had long-span wings, Jumo 213E, armament of two 20-mm MG 151/20 in the wings and an engine-mounted 30-mm MK 108, and a pressurised cockpit. Pre-production H-0 aircraft were similar but with MW-50 injection could boost power to 2,250 hp.

Fw 190 V-18, *Werke* Nr 0040 CF+OY, was next in the development sequence of the C-series and featured a DB 603G engine, a Hirth turbo-blower fed by a large ventral intake, a four-blade VDM propeller and enlarged tail surfaces. This machine was to have a varied career, appearing later as the V-18/U1 with DB 603A-1 and in 1944 as a prototype for the Ta 152H, with a Jumo 213E (V-18/U2).

The production Ta 152H-1 showed few changes from the H-0, although fuel capacity was increased by the use of a 130-gallon tank in the fuselage and five tanks in the wing which together held 88 gallons. Power boosting was via an 18-gallon GM-1 tank in the fuselage and a 15-gallon MW-50 tank in the wing. This increased tankage raised weight considerably. The gross weight of the Ta 152H-1 was 11,508 lb, more than 1,000 lb heavier than the pre-production H-0.

It was not until early 1945 that the Ta 152H was delivered for service, when *Hauptmann* Bruno Stolle's *Erprobungskommando* 152 was formed at Rechlin. The first operational unit to use the Ta 152 was JG 301, commanded by *Oberstleutnant* Fritz Aufhammer, the unit's *Stabsschwarm* operating a small number of aircraft on top cover missions for the rest of the *Geschwader* from March 1945. They were also tasked with protecting Me 262s during take-off and landing as the new jet fighter had proved to be extremely vulnerable to interception by Allied fighters during these times.

Like the Fw 190, the Ta 152 would have been

seen in a number of different forms had the war continued. In letter sequence, the Ta 152A-1 and A-2 projects bore a close resemblance to the Fw 190D and would have carried four MG 151/20 cannon and FuG 24 radio in place of FuG 16, and the similar Ta 152B was to have been used a ground attacker (B-3) and as a heavy fighter (B-4). The second major production variant (after the Ta 152H) was to have been the Ta 152C, the C-1 being powered by a Daimler-Benz DB 603L of 2,100 hp and armed with one MK 108 and four MG 151/20s. Apart from an improved radio fit, the C-2 was similar to the C-1 and the C-3 carried an engine-mounted MK 103 instead of the MK 108. The projected C-4 would have carried WGr 21 rocket launchers. The final Ta 152 variant was the E-1, which was to have been a photo-reconnaissance machine fitted with an Rb 20/30, Rb 50/30 or Rb 75/30 camera. Mention should also be made of the Ta 153, which was a projected high-altitude fighter possessing an airframe similar to the Ta 152C/E fitted to a revised wing. Designed in parallel with the Ta 152, it was abandoned as the need for new jigs would have severely disrupted

An early production Fw 190D-9, *Werke* Nr 210051, fitted with a 66-gallon drop tank. The D-9 was armed with two MG 131 heavy machine-guns above the engine, with two MG 151/20 cannon in the wing roots. It was powered by a Jumo 213A engine delivering 1,750 hp, which could be boosted to 2,240 hp for short periods by using MW-50 water-methanol injection.

fighter production at a critical stage of the war.

During its brief service life, the Ta 152 exhibited performance that was superior to every other piston-engined fighter of the time and pushed the boundaries of propeller-driven fighter technology close to the ultimate. With MW-50 and GM-1 boost it was capable of 472 mph at 41,000 ft and its service ceiling was over 48,000 ft. Owing to its high power and three-blade broad-chord propeller, it could be airborne in a little over 400 yards. The climb rate was around 3,000 ft/min, and the fighter possessed superb acceleration and agility. Indeed, some *Luftwaffe* pilots lucky enough to have flown the Ta 152 preferred it to the Messerschmitt Me 262 jet fighter which, although capable of a maximum speed of 540 mph, was at a distinct disadvantage at slower speeds because of its poor acceleration.

Had it been available a year earlier than it was, the Ta 152 could have severely embarrassed US Eighth Air Force P-51 Mustangs and may well have had some influence on the air battles taking place over the Reich. As it was, its appearance caused little

more than a minor irritation to the Allied air forces. If those in the highest echelons of the German military machine had actively promoted the development and introduction of high performance aircraft instead of relying on the continued production of obsolescent types dating back to the 1930s, the Ta 152 and other advanced projects may well have affected the course of the war.

## Advanced concepts

As with most other fighters of the period, various schemes and proposals were made for the Fw 190 which, for a variety of reasons, were not proceeded with. The amount of drag created by drop tanks mounted on underwing racks led to the development of an overwing tank referred to as the *Doppelreiter* or 'double-rider'. This stemmed from work by *Forschungsgruppe* Graf Zeppelin on a system to evacuate wounded servicemen from the Russian front and featured streamlined tanks blended into the upper surface of the wings, extending beyond the trailing edge. Containing 55 gallons, the frontal area was considerably

**Focke-Wulf Fw 190A-8**
Jagdgeschwader 3
1944

Standard
BMW 801
radial engine
with twin MG 131
machine-guns

This is one of the aircraft that led the way to the definitive Focke-Wulf fighter, the Ta 152. Aircraft V-7, *Werke* Nr 110007 CI+XM, retained the standard wing of the A-8 but with an enlarged tail unit. It was fitted with a DB 603L engine delivering 1,750 hp. The protruding barrels of the wing root MG 151/20 cannon are evident, as is the orifice in the spinner for the engine-mounted 30-mm MK 108 cannon. Two further MG 151/20 cannon were fitted over the engine, firing through the airscrew.

reduced compared to a standard drop tank, and drag was cut appreciably. This came at the expense of degrading the aircraft's handling characteristics however, and the instability produced led to the experiments being abandoned.

An Fw 190B-2 was used to test the Gotha P.56 flying fuel tank in June 1944. The P.56 resembled a small glider, 15 ft 8 in long with a span of 17 ft and a capacity of 143 gallons. It was to be towed by two steel cables up to 22 ft in length. A later version had outriggers attached to the wings of the Fw 190, so that the towed tank could be lowered and its fuel transferred to the 190's own fuel tanks. Not surprisingly perhaps, work was abandoned after several accidents. A development, the P.57, was a glide-bomb designed to be towed behind a Ta 152C in similar fashion to the P.56 but the war ended before trials could take place.

The quest for increased speed and better high altitude performance led to a number of projects being formulated which could have extended Fw 190/Ta 152 development even further. Various engines were considered including the BMW 802, an 18-cylinder air-cooled radial with a projected power of 2,400 hp,

and the 28-cylinder BMW 803 two-row radial of 3,900 hp. Daimler-Benz was also developing new engines that could have powered advanced versions of the Fw 190 and Ta 152. The DB 609 was a 16-cylinder inverted-Vee in-line of 2,660 hp, first bench-tested in 1943, and there were also the 24-cylinder X-type in-line DB 614 of 2,020 hp and the 12-cylinder DB 623 of 2,400 hp. The Junkers Jumo 222 liquid-cooled four-row radial engine of 24 cylinders was also proposed for the Ta 152.

## Jet power proposal

The most radical form of power for the Fw 190 would have been jet propulsion. From 1942 a Focke-Wulf team led by Hans Multhopp had been investigating the feasibility of producing a jet-powered fighter, and this ultimately found expression in the Ta 183 swept-wing project which was to have been powered by a Heinkel-Hirth 109-011A turbojet. A Focke-Wulf designed turbojet was also considered for development and had this gone ahead it would have been flight-tested by replacing the BMW 801 engine in an Fw 190A-3. The likely performance figures would have been a maximum speed of 485 mph with a climb to 40,000 ft in 12 minutes.

# 2. Operational History: 190s in Combat

Although designed as an interceptor fighter, like most classic aircraft the Fw 190 was eventually employed in many differing roles that were far removed from the original service requirement. Outstanding as a fighter, it was equally proficient as a bomber, its weight-lifting ability, speed and range allowing it to be used to strike at distant targets, or as a tactical ground-attack machine in direct support of ground forces. It was highly successful as a bomber-destroyer and for a short time was also used to supplement the *Luftwaffe*'s twin-engined night-fighters.

As already related, the Fw 190A was introduced to service by JG 26. By the summer of 1942 both JG 26 and JG 2 had converted fully. Although aircraft availability at any one time was only around 200, the *Kanalgeschwader* were able to inflict serious losses on their counterparts across the Channel as the RAF hierarchy, in particular Fighter Command's AOC-in-C Air Chief Marshal Sir Sholto Douglas and 11 Group's Air Vice-Marshal Trafford Leigh-Mallory, attempted to draw *Luftwaffe* fighters into a battle of attrition.

The methods used by the RAF included 'Rodeos', the code-name given to pure fighter sweeps, and 'Circus/Ramrod' operations, which involved a relatively small bomber force with large numbers of fighters for protection. Although Fighter Command was stronger numerically, its Spitfire Vs were no match for the Fw 190. The Germans also had the benefit of being able to operate over friendly (or at least occupied) territory, with the added

advantage of excellent radar early warning.

Loss rates were in the order of 4 to 1 in favour of the *Luftwaffe* and by the end of the summer Sholto Douglas had to concede that the Fw 190 was now 'the best all-round fighter in the world'. Despite such an assertion, a few short weeks later the RAF's stock of Spitfire Vs (together with four squadrons of Spitfire IXs and three of Typhoons) were to be pitched into the largest single-day battle of the entire war, one in which it was still hoped to inflict serious damage on the opposing fighter force.

## Landings at Dieppe

On 19 August 1942 elements of the 2nd Canadian Army made an amphibious assault at Dieppe. The landings were intended to test the theory that the best way to launch an invasion of Europe was to seize an existing port facility. The force was to occupy the town and create as much damage as possible before withdrawing later the same day. In the air, Sholto Douglas and Leigh-Mallory looked forward to a decisive victory over the locally based Fw 190As, but it was to be the RAF that suffered the most.

On the German side the day's activities got under way when *Oberleutnant* Horst Sternberg and *Unteroffizier* Peter Crump of 5./JG 26 took off from Abbeville-Drucat at 0620 hrs to carry out a reconnaissance of the Dieppe area. By that time the attack was well under way, and the two had a quick look at the scene below before anti-aircraft fire from their own forces prompted a return to base. Despite the fact that a number of pilots had been given leave, JG 26

Fw 190A-2s of 7./JG 2 at Theville in the summer of 1942. The aircraft to the right of the picture is White 5 and displays the 7th *Staffel's* badge of a thumb pressing on a top hat. Note the protruding barrels of the inboard MG 151/20 cannon and cooling slots behind the exhaust outlet. The rudder and underside of the cowling were in yellow, prompting many RAF fighter pilots to report having been attacked by 'yellow-nosed' Fw 190s.

was able to respond straight away and by the end of the day had flown a total of 377 sorties. Fw 190s of II *Gruppe* were scrambled at 0643 hrs and the first victory of the day went to *Oberfeldwebel* Heinrich Bierwith who shot down Spitfire Vb W3457 flown by *Sous-Lieutenant* Kerlan of 340 Squadron, who baled out successfully and was rescued from the sea.

## British air umbrella

From first light, Fighter Command operated an 'air umbrella' around the landings. In all, 2,122 fighter sorties were flown. Additionally, 266 low-level attack sorties were carried out by Hurricane fighter-bombers, with a further 65 sorties by twin-engined Bostons. In the face of such numerical superiority it was not an easy task for the defending fighters to get at the Hurricanes and Bostons, and most combats were with Spitfires of the fighter screen. By mid

morning another German priority was the protection of Dornier Do 217Es of KG 2 that were engaged in attacking the mass of shipping concentrated in the Channel off Dieppe. On many occasions strafing attacks were also carried out on ground targets.

JG 26 was joined by Fw 190s of JG 2. In the two hours before noon an average of 100 fighters were in the Dieppe area to contest each wing of Spitfires as it arrived. The situation on the ground deteriorated, prompting the withdrawal order to be given at 1000 hrs. The last vessels to leave Dieppe moved off three hours later. By this time the *Jabo Staffeln* of both *Geschwadern* had been in action, attacking shipping targets ranging from landing craft to warships. The most spectacular successes of the day was the sinking of the destroyer HMS *Berkeley* after an attack by two Fw 190s of *Oberleutnant* Fritz Schroter's 10./JG 2.

As the battered Allied force moved away from Dieppe into the Channel, worsening weather began to make life difficult for both sides. The final German victory of the day was recorded by *Oberleutnant* Kurt Ruppert, *Staffelkapitän* of 9./JG 26, who destroyed a Spitfire near Dieppe at 1738 hrs to bring his total for the day to three.

As the activity finally subsided both sides began to take stock. Officially at least, the RAF claimed a victory, but the true picture was that Fighter Command had been out-scored by around 2 to 1. Total RAF losses were 100, including 59 Spitfires, whereas the *Luftwaffe* had lost 48 aircraft of which 23 were fighters.

## Aces in a day

On the German side, the top scorer was *Leutnant* Josef 'Sepp' Wurmheller of 9./JG 2 who claimed a total of seven victories (six Spitfires and one Blenheim) despite the fact that he was suffering from a broken foot and had been concussed during a forced landing on his first sortie. His comrade, *Oberleutnant* Siegfried Schnell, shot down five Spitfires to bring his total to 70. The highest scoring JG 26 pilot was *Oberleutnant* Fulbert Zink who dispatched two Spitfires and a Mustang to equal Kurt Ruppert's total. Other notable successes were two Spitfires claimed by *Geschwader Kommodore Major* Gerhard Schopfel, although the second of these (BL637 flown by Sergeant V. Evans of 222 Squadron) made it back to crash-land at Hawkinge, and two Spitfires shot down by *Oberleutnant* Kurt Ebersberger, leader of the 4th *Staffel*. In all, JG 2 claimed 59 victories and JG 26 38. On the debit side, JG 2 lost fourteen aircraft and eight pilots killed, including the *Kommodore* of I Gruppe, *Oberleutnant* Erich Leie, who was forced to bale out wounded from his Fw 190A-3 (*Werke* Nr 0326). JG 26 fared a little better, losing seven aircraft (including one Bf 109G) and six pilots.

The raid itself had been a complete failure and even the hoped for aerial victory had not materialised. Although the effectiveness of the

Pilots and ground crews take a break before the next scramble. Just discernible on this Fw 190A-4, possibly of II./JG 26, is a small triangular antenna post mounted on top of the fin, indicating a change from FuG 7 to FuG 16 radio. Unlike many Fw 190s of the time, the outer MG FF cannon have been retained.

Ground crews attached to JG 2 go about their business, taking advantage of the warm French summer to top up their suntans at the same time. The large rear-hinged panel which gave access to the fuselage-mounted MG 17 machine-guns is evident – as are the potentially disastrous repercussions should it ever blow back during flight. The narrow headrest armour suggests an early A-series aircraft.

German fighter force had been reduced by the end of the day, a total of nearly 200 aircraft were available again the next day as unserviceable machines were brought back on line. Stocks of ammunition, which had nearly been exhausted, were quickly replaced.

One aspect of the Dieppe fiasco, which tended to be overlooked at the time, was a somewhat ineffectual attack by Eighth Air Force B-17 Flying Fortresses on the airfield at Abbeville-Drucat. Little damage was done and no interceptions were made since the locally based fighters were fully occupied over Dieppe,

but this was a portent of things to come. The bomber-destroyer role would become the Fw 190's primary mission as the raids grew in intensity. The first US loss to fighter action took place on 6 September 1942, when a B-17F (41-24445) of the 97th Bomb Group was shot down by *Hauptmann* Conny Meyer of II./JG 26 during a raid on the Potez works at Amiens.

## Serious bomber threat

Gone was the luxury of being able to ignore the RAF's Circus operations. The destructive power of the American heavy bombers meant that every raid had to be contested. The size of the B-17s and B-24s caused initial problems, as pilots found it difficult to get into a suitable position to attack. Problems were also experienced in assessing the correct range to open fire. Return fire from the bomber formations during attacks from the rear was formidable, so much so that head-on attacks began to be experimented with.

Towards the end of 1942 a set of guidelines was issued to fighter units that implored pilots to maintain their *Schwarm* formations so that more than one attack could be carried out. This was easier said than done, however. In the face of the concentrated barrage put up by American gunners, it is easy to understand why many pilots chose to break away to lower levels by half rolling and diving – a manoeuvre known to the Germans as *die Abschwung* and to the Americans as the Split-S.

## Anti-bomber tactics

Over the following months tactics varied, some units preferring to attack from the front, while others favoured the classic curve of pursuit. The former method required much higher levels of flying skill, together with excellent shooting ability and accurate assessment of range, qualities which were often beyond the inexperienced newcomers who formed the majority of *Jagdwaffe* pilots in the last two years of the war. This, together with the ever increasing number of bombers, led to the introduction of specialised units whose task was to deliver concentrated attacks using heavily armed fighters, typically the Fw 190A-6 and A-7 armed with two MG 131 machine-guns and four MG 151/20s in the wings.

The ultimate *Sturmbock* was the A-8/R8, which had the two outer MG 151s replaced by 30-mm MK 108s. The amount of armour carried increased significantly. In addition to the cowling ring and pilot protection of the standard A-8, the A-8/R8 also had extra plating applied to the cockpit sides and cannon magazines, and thicker canopy side panels. The outboard MK 108s were the primary armament, three hits from this weapon usually being enough to destroy a four-engined bomber or *Viermot*. On average, twenty hits were needed with 20-mm ammunition.

Tactical formations were revised, and each *Staffel* flew in a broad arrow formation with minimal distance between aircraft. Assuming that the leader could get his force into position behind the bombers at close range, it was relatively easy, even for inexperienced pilots, to

down a B-17 or B-24. To achieve such a situation there had to be almost flawless ground control and the American escort fighters had to be dealt with by the *Sturmgruppe*'s own escort. Otherwise the bomber-destroyers, weighed down by armour and heavy guns, would be at a severe disadvantage.

## Storm units

The first unit to be formed, *Sturmstaffel* 1, was commanded by *Major* Hans-Gunter von Kornatski, and began its work-up period at Achmer late in 1943. By the New Year, fourteen Fw 190A-6 aircraft were on strength of which eleven were operational. Soon afterwards, the unit moved to Dortmund and flew its first mission on 5 January 1944. On this occasion, no contact was made with B-17s attacking the

Fw 190A-4 *Werke* Nr 5735 of 8./JG 2 having its batteries recharged. A photo from this angle gives an excellent view of the radio sternpost. The aircraft also has bulged panels on the inner wing surfaces, added to make room for the breeches of the MG 151/20 cannon. The aircraft is probably a late-model A-4, as it features the widened headrest armour that was introduced during the production run of this series.

An Fw 190A-4 of I./JG 54 *Grunherz*, the 'Green Hearts' *Geschwader*. This unit counted such famous *Experten* as Nowotny, Kittel and Rudorffer among its number. This aircraft is resplendent in its winter camouflage – already heavily stained by the exhaust – and again features widened headrest armour. Clearly evident is the bulged fairing under the wing associated with the outer MG FF cannon.

shipyards at Kiel. Combat experience over the next few weeks meant that by early March the unit, which was now based at Salzwedel between Hamburg and Berlin, was able to inflict serious damage.

## Battle over Berlin

On 6 March 1944, 730 Eighth Air Force heavy bombers took off from their bases in East Anglia heading for Berlin. This was the first mass daylight raid on the German capital flown in daylight, though the actual first raid had taken place two days before when a small number of B-17s which had not heeded a recall had reached the city. The bombers were escorted by fighters drawn from nineteen USAAF Fighter Groups, plus two squadrons of RAF Mustangs. Faced with such overwhelming odds the *Luftwaffe* had little option but to concentrate its forces. Use of the so-called *Gefechtsverband* (battle formation) made up from a large number of fighters of different types and/or variants, each with a specific task, ensured that the carnage in the ensuing air battle was on a scale never previously seen.

*Sturmstaffel* 1 was airborne at 1130 hrs. In the vicinity of Magdeburg it joined up with Bf 110 and Me 410 twin-engined heavy fighters of II and III./ZG 26 and I and II./ZG 76, together with Bf 109s and Fw 190s of I, II and IV./JG 3. The resulting *Gefechtsverband* comprised over 100 fighters. An hour later the first bombers were seen. These were B-17s of the 1st Bomb Division on their way to the primary target, the Erkner ball bearing works. The initial wave of WGr 21-equipped Bf 110s and Me 410s was not particularly effective, as most of the mortars exploded short of their intended target, but the subsequent head-on attack by the aircraft of JG 3 shot down several B-17s and caused enough damage in others that they were forced to leave the protection of their comrades.

At the same time the pilots of *Sturmstaffel* 1 were manoeuvring to begin their own attack from the rear. The problems that the pilots faced were many. The overtake speed of their heavily laden fighters was not great, and all the time they spent overhauling the bombers they were subject to continuous defensive fire. There was also the threat posed by the American

Fw 190G-3s, possibly of II./SG 10. The G-3 was a ground-attack variant of the 190. Both aircraft seen here carry ETC 501 bomb racks under the fuselage, but only 'M' is fitted with Focke-Wulf produced under-wing racks. For long-range missions an SC 500 bomb and two 66-gallon drop tanks were usually carried, but for targets where range was not a consideration the under-wing tanks could be replaced by two SC 250 bombs.

escort fighters which, if they ever got through the *Sturmstaffel*'s own escort, were likely to wreak havoc among the unwieldy Fw 190s. Even assuming that they got through unscathed, there were difficulties caused by wake turbulence and condensation trails streaming back from the bombers.

## Bomber engagement

The approach was usually carried out in a shallow dive to keep the speed up as much as possible. The fact that the attack was performed by a number of aircraft in relatively close formation meant that defensive fire from the bombers was not as concentrated as it would be in the case of an individual or pair attack.

*Sturmstaffel* 1 engaged the Fortresses of the 91st Bomb Group at 1235 hrs, and within sixty seconds two B-17s had fallen to the guns of *Unteroffizier* Kurt Rohrich and *Leutnant* Gerhard Dost. Another was forced to leave the formation (an achievement credited as a *Herausschuss*) when attacked by *Unteroffizier* Willi Maximowitz, and not long after *Feldwebel* Hermann Wahlfeld destroyed another B-17. The final confirmed 'kill' in the initial wave of attacks went to *Oberleutnant* Othmar Zehart, although a further B-17 went down having been hit by an Fw 190 which pressed in so close that it ripped off part of the bomber's tailplane.

Much has been made of the declaration that had to be signed by *Sturmstaffel* pilots that they would ram an enemy bomber if they were unable to bring it down by more conventional means. However, the number of deliberate ramming attacks were few as the Fw 190's weight of fire at close range was usually sufficient to cripple a heavy bomber without

A crashed Fw 190D-9 of *Stabsschwarm JG 4* at Rhein-Main. It carries Defence of the Reich bands around the tail and the chevron and two vertical bars of a *Major beim Stab* (Major attached to the *Jagdgeschwader* staff).

recourse to such drastic measures. Later in the day two more B-17s were shot down by *Leutnant* Werner Gerth, but the unit's most successful day to date had to be set against the loss of Gerhard Dost who was shot down and killed by P-51 Mustangs near Salzwedel.

## Mixed fortunes

Although the *Sturmstaffel* had acquitted itself well, other units were not so fortunate, particularly the *Zerstörer Geschwader* which lost sixteen aircraft in total. Seven single-engined fighters were also lost, including two Fw 190s. Total German losses for the day amounted to eighty-seven fighters, with thirty-six aircrew killed and a further twenty-seven wounded. For their part the Americans suffered the loss of sixty-nine heavies, making the Berlin raid of 6 March one of the most costly of the war.

The *Sturmstaffel* continued to see action until it was disbanded at the end of April 1944, and had its most successful day shortly before it was broken up. On 29 April the USAAF launched another major attack on Berlin but on this occasion events conspired to present the defenders with a golden opportunity. The bomber stream became widely dispersed, which made the escort fighters' job impossible.

A navigation error by one of the Bomb Wings put it forty miles off track. Taking full advantage, the Fw 190s of the *Sturmstaffel* came in from behind shortly after IV./JG 3 had attacked from head-on. In only five minutes eight B-17s were shot down, with another five receiving damage sufficiently serious for them to be forced out of formation. Most pilots were able to claim either a 'kill' or a *Herauschuss*, including *Unteroffizier* Kurt Rohrich who claimed his ninth victim, *Leutnant* Siegfried Muller whose score rose to six and *Leutnant* Werner Gerth who shot down one and severely damaged another to bring his tally to eight.

*Sturmstaffel* 1's main claim to fame was that it had proved the theory. The decision was made to expand the force by creating two new *Sturmgruppen*, II.(*Sturm*)/JG 3 and II.(*Sturm*)/JG 300 which, together with IV.(*Sturm*)/JG 3, hammered away at the American daylight raids for the rest of the year. The Fw 190 proved to be the ideal machine for use as a heavy fighter, its adaptability, ruggedness and inherent structural strength being ideally suited to the role. Sadly its fine handling qualities had been squeezed out by the weight of armour and weaponry that it had been forced to carry, but if it managed to stay

Captured by US forces early in 1945, Fw 190D-9 'White 15' is most probably ex-JG 26. The long nose of the D-series covered a powerful Junkers Jumo in-line engine in place of the compact BMW radial of earlier variants.

out of the reach of escorting Mustangs its survivability was surprisingly high. As the Fw 190 piled on the weight, many pilots were to applaud Kurt Tank's decision to build the undercarriage far stronger than he needed to.

## Pocket-sized load carrier

The 190's ability to carry a heavy load of bombs and/or overload fuel tanks with ease soon led to its use as a fighter-bomber. The first unit to become operational was 10 (*Jabo*)/JG 26, which handed over its Bf 109F-4/R1s and began conversion to the Fw 190A-2/U3 and A-3/U3 in June 1942. The Fw 190 proved to be much more suited to ground attack than the Messerschmitt 109. It was faster, handled better and was much more stable on the ground with a bomb load attached. It could also carry double the load of the Bf 109F.

Attacks were carried out on targets along the south coast and on shipping in the English Channel. These raids proved almost impossible for the British to stop, as the Fw 190s invariably came in at high speed and low level so that radar early warning was usually non-existent.

Unless they stumbled upon the 190s with height advantage, Fighter Command's Spitfire Vs had little chance of catching let alone shooting down any of the attacking aircraft, so the main deterrent to such activity lay in anti-aircraft defences – which were to claim the majority of the *Jabos* that were lost. The hazards of such missions were highlighted on 30 July when the *Jabostaffel's Kapitän, Oberleutnant* Hans-Joachim Geburtig, was hit by flak during an attack on shipping in Littlehampton harbour and drowned during the subsequent ditching.

Hit and run attacks were to continue for the rest of the year and beyond, eventually becoming such a concern that the RAF had to resort to using standing patrols and basing fast Hawker Typhoons in areas that were most vulnerable.

One of the largest attacks took place on 31 October 1942 against Canterbury, and was intended as a reprisal for raids being carried out on German cities by Bomber Command. Even with the *Jabos* of 10./JG 2, the dedicated fighter-bomber force in the west amounted to only nineteen serviceable aircraft, so to

One of a number of German aircraft tested by the US after the war, this Fw 190D-9 carries the Foreign Evaluation number FE-121. The bulged hood used by most late-war Fw 190 variants is visible, as are the wide-chord propeller blades and the ram air intake for the supercharger.

strengthen this meagre force many standard Fw 190 fighters were modified to carry bombs. The attack was carried out in the evening under a leaden overcast, which severely hampered the efforts of defending Spitfires. After making a landfall near Deal, the 190s headed for the cathedral city of Canterbury where they bombed indiscriminately, damaging many buildings and killing 32 people. The British defences were taken completely by surprise, and only one Fw 190A-2 of II./JG 2 was shot down. Its pilot, *Feldwebel* Alfred Hell, survived to become a PoW.

For JG 26, the only mishap over England occurred when *Unteroffizier* Alfred Immervoll lost a wingtip when he struck a balloon cable, but it suffered a major blow over France on its return. *Leutnant* Paul Galland was shot down and killed by a Spitfire V flown by Flying Officer R.G.V. Gibbs of 91 Squadron, who had followed the attacking aircraft back across the Channel. Galland had attempted to go to the aid of another Fw 190 that Gibbs was firing at, but low cloud gave the RAF pilot the opportunity to get behind Galland and shoot

him down in flames. His moment of glory was to be short lived, however, as Galland's No. 2, *Feldwebel* Johann Edmann, quickly dispatched Gibbs, who was also killed.

## Jabos over London

A more audacious operation was planned for 20 January 1943, which was to be the largest daylight raid on the UK since 1940. Following an early morning reconnaissance in which *Leutnant* Hans Kummerling of 8./JG 26 was shot down by a Typhoon of 609 Squadron, 90 fighter and fighter-bombers (including the Bf 109Gs of 6./JG 26) attacked London in three waves. The first wave, comprising the *Jabo Staffeln* of JG 2 and 26 (together with elements of the *Stab* and I./JG 26 as escort), achieved complete surprise and dropped their bombs on the docks area, although some went astray and hit a school in Greenwich killing 38 children. The only losses from this wave were the Fw 190A-4 of *Leutnant* Hermann Koch who was hit by light flak and had to crash-land in a field, and the similar machine of *Oberfeldwebel* Paul Kierstein who was shot down by the Spitfire IX

The Fw 190/Ju 88 *Mistel* (Mistletoe) was a combination which Germany hoped to use to knock out high profile targets. This trainer was used to acquaint pilots with the composite's handling characteristics. For training the Fw 190's undercarriage was left down as it was not possible to lower the gear with the Ju 88 still attached.

of Wing Commander Dickie Milne, leader of the Biggin Hill Wing.

The second wave contained some of JG 2's Fw 190 fighters equipped with fragmentation bombs, but by now virtually every available RAF fighter in the immediate area was in the air and most of the 190's jettisoned their loads near the south coast and turned for home. *Feldwebel* Alfred Barthel of 5./JG 26 was shot down by a Spitfire of 340 Squadron but the most serious losses were to the Bf 109G-4s of 6./JG 26 who had two pilots killed with two more shot down to become PoWs.

The third wave comprised the *Stabsschwarm* and III./JG 26 led by *Major* Priller who provided cover, the 7th *Staffel's Oberleutnant* Klaus Mietusch claiming two Spitfires. A number of III *Gruppe* aircraft returned very low on fuel and *Unteroffizier* Robert Hager was injured when he crash-landed his Fw 190A-4

(*Werke* Nr 7102) at Calais-Marck.

As JG 2 had also lost one pilot killed with another injured, the operation had proved to be extremely costly, and was not repeated. The *Jabos* continued to harass British defences. On 9 April 1943 the fighter-bomber *Staffeln* of JG 2 and 26 were merged to form 10./SKG 10, which turned its attention to night attacks.

## Fw 190 *Jabos* in the East

As a ground-attack machine the Fw 190 was to come into its own on the Russian Front. The A-series had been introduced in the east by I./JG 51 in September 1942 and it had also been used operationally by I and II./ SchG 1 from early 1943. The Fw 190 was far better suited to the primitive conditions that had to be endured in Russia than the Bf 109. Its wide-track undercarriage, its ease of handling on the ground and its ability to stay in the air after

The Fw 190/Ju 88 composite that formed part of the collection of captured German aircraft exhibited at Farnborough in 1945. On operations the Fw 190 normally carried a 264-gallon drop tank under the fuselage and used fuel from the Ju 88 during the outward flight.

receiving considerable punishment from ground fire led to most fighter-bomber pilots preferring the radial-engined machine to the Messerschmitts that most had flown previously.

## Stuka replacement

Following the battle of Kursk in July 1943, there was a major reorganisation of the fighter-bomber units that saw them join with the *Stukageschwader* (dive-bomber groups) and the *Schnellkampf-geschwader* (fast bomber groups) under a unified command, with a simplified abbreviation of SG (*Schlachtgeschwader*). It was at this point that the Junkers Ju 87 began to be phased out in favour of the Fw 190F and G, which could lift an equivalent or even bigger bomb load, while at the same time offering the air combat ability to deal with Russian fighters if the need arose.

Indeed, II./SG 2 (formerly II./SchG 1) claimed 247 victories in the air during the first six months of 1944, the most notable claimant being *Leutnant* August Lambert who accounted for over a third of this total. Lambert was killed shortly before the end of the war on 17 April 1945 by which time he held the rank of

*Oberleutnant* as leader of 8./SG 77 and had been credited with the destruction of 116 aircraft.

Weapons used for ground attack included standard SC 250 and 500 bombs carried under the fuselage, or four SC 50s under the wings. AB 250 containers with SD-2, SD-4 or SD-10 bomblets were used against soft-skinned targets. Towards the end of the war *Panzerblitz* air-to-ground rockets came into use.

## Attacking ground targets

The tactics employed usually involved approaching the target at around 7,000 ft before, if numbers allowed, splitting into two separate formations. One group would then bomb in a 60–70 degree dive, followed by a pull up to protect the second wave as they commenced their attack. Aerial combat was avoided if at all possible, and if Russian fighters tried to intervene, bombs and overload fuel tanks would be jettisoned before diving to escape at full speed. When faced with enemy tanks, pilots would carry out ultra low-level attacks from around 20–30 ft, dropping their bombs as the tank disappeared from view under the nose. A one second delay was

In the last months of the war the advancing Russian forces acquired many German aircraft including a number of Fw 190D-9s. These were tested alongside contemporary Soviet fighters and some captured D-9s are reputed to have been flown by Soviet pilots over Berlin immediately before the German collapse.

enough to ensure that the aircraft escaped the blast as the bomb detonated.

Although the Fw 190 was the most capable ground-attack machine in the *Luftwaffe*'s inventory, the pressure being exerted on all fronts was such that it could not be deployed in large numbers. Losses were proportionately severe as a result. The replacement of the Ju 87 was not complete until mid-1944. Even then, the seven Fw 190-equipped *Schlachtgruppen* in the east could only put up around 200 machines at any one time.

## Mediterranean theatre

It was a similar situation in the Mediterranean. The first Fw 190s to see action in this theatre were the fighters of II./JG 2. These had been hurriedly transferred from north-western France to reinforce German defences following the Allied landings in North Africa (code-named 'Torch') on 8 November 1942. Their stay was to be short-lived, and the main fighter-

bomber response during the actions over Sicily, Salerno and Anzio came via the Fw 190A-4/U8s of SKG 10 and SG 2 which attempted to stem the tide by attacking troop movements and shipping. Despite mounting losses in the face of Allied air superiority, the Fw 190 *Jabos* continued to harass Allied ground forces as they made slow progress towards Rome. One of the worst days for SKG 10 occurred on 21 May 1944 when Spitfires of 145 Squadron, led by Squadron Leader Neville Duke, shot down eight Fw 190s out of a force of twenty.

As well as its day-fighter and ground-attack roles, the Fw 190 was also used as a makeshift night-fighter. The 'Wilde Sau' or 'Wild Boar' tactics were devised by *Major* Hajo Herrmann after Bomber Command's use of 'Window' to swamp German radars from July 1943. *Wilde Sau* used single-seat fighters to provide an additional line of defence by attacking RAF heavy bombers visually over the target area. Lacking radar, the day-fighters needed light to

A single Fw 190A-5 was sent to Japan for evaluation purposes, but no production was undertaken.

be able to spot their targets: luckily the light they needed was provided by the fires on the ground below, together with illumination from searchlights and even from the flares dropped by the British Pathfinders.

Again thanks to its wide-track landing gear the Fw 190 was more suited to the night-fighter role than the Bf 109, but despite some initial success, losses through accidents began to mount. Eventually more advanced radars and different tactics adopted by twin-engined fighters led to single-seat night-fighters being withdrawn. Despite this, experiments were carried out in 1944 with Fw 190s equipped with *Neptun* radar equipment and some success was achieved by NJGr.10 and NJG 11.

## *Mistel* composite bomber

One of the more outlandish uses of Kurt Tank's masterpiece was as the upper component of the *Mistel* combination. In this, a single-engined fighter was mounted above an explosive-packed Ju 88. In later versions, the bomber's crew compartment was fitted with a 7,800 lb explosive warhead. Initial experiments resulted in the *Mistel* 1, comprising a Ju 88A-4/Bf 109F-4, that was used to attack shipping in the English Channel in August 1944. An improved *Mistel* 2 version, which employed an Fw 190A-6 or F-8 mated to a Ju 88G-1, was intended to knock out several power stations which were a

vital supplier to the Soviet armaments industry. However, by the time these weapons could be made ready, the advances made by the Russian armies had put these targets out of range. Final variants of the *Mistel* combines were the 3A (Ju 88A-4/FW 190A-8), 3B (Ju 88H-4/Fw 190A-8) and 3C (Ju 88G-10/Fw 190F-8). Although the primary mission was no longer possible, the *Mistels* were used instead to attack the Görlitz bridges over the Neisse on 9 March 1945 and later in the month against bridges over the Rhine and Vistula. The final *Mistel* attack occurred on 16 April when a number of Soviet bridgeheads were targeted.

## Limited overseas sales

Although the need for fighter aircraft to defend the homeland was great, the Fw 190 was exported in small numbers commencing with the sale of 72 A-3s to Turkey in 1943. These aircraft were supplied in the early *Luftwaffe* desert camouflage scheme of mottled brown/green. The armament was restricted to two MG 17 machine-guns mounted over the engine and two MG FF cannon in the outer wings. The wing root guns were deleted.

The Fw 190s were used by the 3rd and 5th Squadrons of the 5th Regiment, Turkish Air Force and were often flown alongside Spitfire Vs that had been supplied in 1944. Both types remained in service until at least 1948.

A Japanese test pilot prepares to fly the Fw 190A-5. The aircraft has the standard armament of two engine-mounted MG 17 machine-guns, two wing root MG 151/20 cannon, with two MG FF cannon outboard. Although noted for its build quality, this particular example of the Fw 190 appears to be rather second-hand, judging by the fit of the cowling panels.

A number of Fw 190As were flown in Romania by the *Aeronautica Regal Romana* prior to that country's change of allegiance in mid-1944, and around 70 Fw 190F-8s were also supplied to the Hungarian Air Force. The first of these aircraft were delivered in early November 1944 and took part in ground-attack missions against Russian forces later in the month. Operations continued until 1945.

## Captured 190s

During the war various examples of the Fw 190 fell into Russian hands, the first being an A-4 of JG 54 which force-landed in Soviet territory in June 1943. It was tested by the NII VVS (Research Test Institute of the Air Force) who were rather disappointed with its performance, although this may well have been because of its poor condition. The A-5, A-8 and F-8 were also tested, as were a number of long-nosed D-9s captured shortly before the end of hostilities. Once again the Russians were not impressed,

rating the D-9 as having only 'fair' performance. It has been suggested that some of these aircraft appeared over Berlin immediately prior to the cessation of hostilities. During the war a single Fw 190A-5 was delivered to Japan for evaluation and, although no further interest was shown by the Japanese, the Allies still thought it necessary to give the code-name 'Fred' to the Fw 190, just in case.

## French service

The Fw 190 was one of the many German types used in the rebirth of the French Air Force in 1945. French-built examples designated NC 900 were produced by the SNCAC and were pressed into use. This was something of a desperate measure, as the French production line had been frequently sabotaged during the war, and many problems were encountered when the aircraft was put in service. Concerns over reliability and safety led to the NC 900 quickly being replaced by other types.

Above and below: The Fw 190 was one of the types used to reform the French Air Force in the immediate post-war period. The Germans had set up a production line in France, and after the war 64 Fw 190A-8s were produced under the designation NC 900 by SNCAC at Cavant. No. 37, seen above, is inhabiting a somewhat untidy dispersal area. The NC 900 was in service only for a short period and was soon discarded.

# 3. Fw 190 People: Engineers and Aces

Many men were to make their name on the Fw 190. Some were to use it in combat to accumulate high scores, whereas others could reflect that they had produced one of the finest fighters of its generation, one that left rival manufacturers with an extremely difficult task in matching its performance, let alone surpassing it.

Although no one single individual could ever be responsible for the creation of a complex military aircraft, the name of Kurt Tank stands out above all others. Tank was born on 24 February 1898 in Bromberg in West Prussia and studied electrical engineering at the Technical High School in Berlin. An early interest in aerodynamics developed to the point where he was sufficiently skilled to design a glider, which was built and flown (by Tank himself) in 1923. On leaving further education his first job was as an aerodynamicist with the Rohrbach Aircraft Works.

During his six years with the company Tank was responsible for the hull design of several of the company's flying boats, and during this period he also learned to fly, becoming a very able pilot. On leaving in 1929 he worked for a short time with Bayerische Flugzeugwerke before joining Focke-Wulf at Bremen in 1931 as Chief of the Design Office.

Kurt Tank's first design for Focke-Wulf was the Fw 56 *Stosser*, a single-seat high-wing monoplane trainer first built in 1933. It possessed superb aerobatic qualities and its clean lines endowed it with a high diving speed, a performance feature that further influenced Ernst Udet who was fast becoming an advocate of the dive-bomber. Subsequent designs supervised by Tank included a number of twin-engined machines such as the Fw 58 *Weihe* communications and light transport, the Fw 187 *Falke* fighter that was rated by many as superior to the Bf 110, and the Fw 189 *Uhu* short-range reconnaissance aircraft. Tank was also responsible for the Fw 159 single-seat fighter that competed with the Bf 109 and the Fw 200 *Condor* that first achieved fame with Lufthansa before it was used as a long-range anti-shipping aircraft.

## Designed for pilots

As an extremely competent pilot, Tank could easily appreciate the feedback that he received from his team of test pilots who were led by Hans Sander. Sander was also proficient in more than one aspect of his work, as he had initially studied mechanical engineering at the Technical High School at Aachen in the late 1920s. It was around this time that he found an interest in aeronautics, becoming a qualified pilot, and he also designed and built a high performance glider during his studies.

The next stage in his education was at the Research Institute for Aeronautics in Berlin, where he took a three-year course as a *Flugbaumeister* (Project Engineer). This included a fifteen-month spell at the *Luftwaffe* test centre at Rechlin, where he flew many different types of aircraft. Having successfully completed the course, he was taken on as a development test pilot by Focke-Wulf in April 1937.

Kurt Tank (left) shares an obviously amusing tale with Focke-Wulf test pilot Dipl Ing Karl Mehlhorn. Tank was adamant that his team of test pilots should also be qualified engineers so that expertise in technical matters would complement their piloting skills to smooth the Fw 190's development.

Sander took the Fw 190 on its maiden flight on 1 June 1939, and was to play a major role in its subsequent development. His abilities both as pilot and engineer led to an attempt to develop a rudimentary ejector seat activated by an explosive charge. Ground trials were carried out with an Fw 190A-0 and although the device worked, it was calculated that the charge would not be enough for the seat to clear the tailplane when flying at high speed. As Sander was fully committed to the test programme on the Fw 190 and could not spare time to develop the system, it was quietly forgotten about.

The trials and tribulations of the Fw 190 development programme have already been related in Chapter 1. The type might well have been dropped had it not been for the enthusiastic lobbying of *Oberleutnant*s Otto

Behrens and Karl Borris of JG 26, who flight-tested the machine in the spring of 1941. Both had joined the *Luftwaffe* pre-war as mechanics before transferring to flying duties, and recent combat experience ensured that they had a vested interest in making the Fw 190 work. Behrens was to survive a bale out on 24 March 1942 when he was shot down by Flying Officer Hugo 'Sinker' Armstrong of 129 Squadron near Abbeville, but was injured on landing. Following this incident it was decided that his technical abilities could best be used elsewhere and three months later he was transferred to Rechlin where he remained for the rest of the conflict, eventually becoming its *Kommodore*. In the immediate post-war years Behrens lived in Argentina where he was killed test flying Kurt Tank's I.Ae.33 Pulqui II jet fighter.

An early production Fw 190A-1 about to be taken on a test flight. The retractable stirrup used to gain access to the cockpit can be seen to the right of the undercarriage leg.

Karl Borris was to achieve fame as the only officer to fly continuously with JG 26 throughout the war, having arrived on 1 December 1939. Despite an inauspicious start on 13 May 1940, when he was shot down by a Defiant of 264 Squadron, he ended the war with 43 victories, of which 36 were achieved with the Fw 190. One of the worst moments of his long career occurred on 14 May 1943 when he was forced to bale out at around 22,000 ft after his Fw 190A-5 (*Werke* Nr 7326) was hit by return fire from a B-17. Although his parachute appeared to open normally, it then partially collapsed and Borris was badly injured when he hit the ground, necessitating a lengthy period of convalescence in hospital. He ended the war as *Kommodore* of I./JG 26 with the rank of *Major*.

By the time that the Fw 190 was introduced to service by II./JG 26, the *Gruppe* could boast a number of aces, many of whom would increase their scores significantly with their new mount. Its 4th, 5th and 6th *Staffeln* were led by *Oberleutnant*s Kurt Ebersberger, Wolfgang Kosse and Walter Schneider respectively.

## Spitfire shootdown

Ebersberger had joined JG 26 before the war and had claimed his first victim on 15 August 1940 when he shot down a Spitfire over Tonbridge. By the time that he came to the Fw 190 his score had risen to eleven and his first operational sortie in the new type on 17 September 1941 resulted in a 'kill' when he destroyed a Spitfire near Boulogne. After a short spell as an instructor with *Jagdgruppe Ost* in the spring of 1943, Ebersberger returned to JG 26 as *Kapitän* of the 8th *Staffel* but was killed

An early pre-production Fw 190A-0, one of a number of airframes that were retained by the manufacturer and used for development work. It is seen here fitted with a 300-litre (66-gallon) drop tank.

on 24 October 1943 when he baled out too low after having been attacked and hit by an RAF Mustang of 400 Squadron. His victory tally at the time stood at thirty.

The career of Wolfgang Kosse was to be anything but straightforward. He had been given command of the 5./JG 26 on 22 August 1941, achieving a total of eleven victories before departing for JG 5 in Norway in May 1942. His promotion to *Hauptmann* was dramatically reversed after he damaged an aircraft during an unauthorised flight, and he joined *Sturmstaffel* 1 in late 1943 having been demoted to *Flieger* or private. He eventually regained his rank but was posted missing on 24 December 1944 when leader of 13./JG 3, with twenty-eight victories to his name.

## Non-combat loss

Walter Schneider's use of the Fw 190 was to be brief, as he and four other pilots were killed on 22 December 1941 when they encountered bad weather during a flight from Wevelghem airfield to Abbeville-Drucat, crashing into high ground. At the time of his death Schneider had twenty confirmed kills.

The last major action of 1941 occurred on 8

November when the RAF launched Circus 110, a co-ordinated strike on a distillery at St Pol and the marshalling yard at Lille. Things went badly wrong almost from the start, and JG 26 was able to take full advantage. Difficulties with a missed rendezvous and straggling resulted in fourteen Spitfires being shot down, seven of which were claimed by the pilots of II *Gruppe*. *Hauptmann* Joachim Muncheberg, commanding officer of the *Gruppe*, shot down two to bring his total of victories to 59, and there were single successes for *Oberleutnant* Kurt Ebersberger, *Feldwebel* Adolf Glunz, *Oberleutnant* Koch and *Oberfeldwebel*s Walter Meyer and Wilhelm Mackenstedt. All but the latter were already aces by the time of this combat (Mackenstedt had to wait until early 1943). Muncheberg's score had risen to 83 by the time he left JG 26 in July 1942 – he eventually became leader of JG 77 but was killed in North Africa in combat with USAAF Spitfires on 23 March 1943. His tally at the time stood at 135. 'Addi' Glunz was to remain with the *Schlageter Geschwader* until March 1945 by which time he had been promoted to become leader of the 6th *Staffel* and had been credited with 71 victories.

This A-5/U8 carries a typical weapons load for an Fw 190 *Jabo-Rei* (long-range fighter-bomber) mission. The primary weapon is a 500-kg (1,102-lb) SC 500 bomb on the centreline ETC 501 rack, with two 300-litre (66-gallon) drop tanks under the wings. The outer wing cannon have been removed to leave two MG 151/20s in the wing roots. Aft of the access stirrup are the FuG 16 D/F loop aerial and the whip aerial for FuG 25 IFF.

By the end of November 1941, Fw 190s were issued to JG 26's III *Gruppe*, then commanded by *Major* Gerhard Schopfel although he was shortly to take over as *Geschwader Kommodore* from *Oberstleutnant* Adolf Galland on the latter's departure as Inspector of Fighters. Schopfel was another long-standing member of JG 26 and was to remain as its leader until early January 1943, his score steadily rising during this period to 45.

## 'Pips' Priller in command

Schopfel's position as leader of III *Gruppe* was taken by the charismatic *Hauptmann* Josef 'Pips' Priller whose abilities as a combat leader were matched by his ebullient nature on the ground. Perhaps more than any other, Priller was to be the driving force behind JG 26 throughout the war, his dynamic leadership proving to be an inspiration to those around him. He was to take over as *Kommodore* from Schopfel and led JG 26 for the next two years, leaving in January 1945 to replace Adolf Galland as Inspector of Fighters. His final victory tally stood at 101.

A lack of activity in early 1942 allowed the remaining elements of JG 26 to convert to the Fw 190 including *Hauptmann* Johannes Seifert's

I *Gruppe*. Seifert had notched up his first victory on 10 May 1940, the day that the so-called 'Phoney War' had come to an end, shooting down a Fokker D.21 near Rotterdam. He had fought in the Battle of Britain and by the time he came to the Fw 190 had increased his score to 24. Seifert was to lead I *Gruppe*'s brief foray into Russia in January 1943 (replacing III./JG 54) but was given a staff post in Bulgaria the following June. Following a personal appeal to Adolf Galland, Seifert returned to JG 26 on 9 September 1943, taking over as *Kommodore* of II *Gruppe*. Not long after, on 25 November, his Fw 190A-6 collided with a P-38 Lightning which was to count as his 57th and last victory.

JG 26's monopoly of the Fw 190 ended in March 1942 when first JG 2 and then JG 1 began to receive A-2s. JG 2 had the job of defending north-west France, and the arrival of the Fw 190 in this area came as a nasty shock for Fighter Command's 10 Group whose pilots had only seen the Focke-Wulf during occasional operations from 11 Group bases. British loss rates began to rise dramatically, and several RAF squadrons had to be withdrawn from the firing line to recuperate. JG 2 was led by *Oberstleutnant* Walter Oesau and had many other *Experten* within its ranks, including *Hauptmann* Erich Leie of I *Gruppe* and *Hauptmann* Hans 'Assi' Hahn of III *Gruppe*. Oesau was a veteran of the conflict in Spain and had also served with JG 3 and JG 51. His final post was as *Kommodore* of JG 1 and, like Seifert before him, was killed in combat with USAAF P-38s in May 1944, by which time he had amassed 125 kills. Two other high scoring JG 2 pilots of this period were *Oberleutnant* Egon Mayer, *Kapitän* of the 7th *Staffel*, and *Oberleutnant* Siegfried Schnell, leader of the 9th *Staffel*. Mayer would be another to achieve his century, with 102 victories at the time of his death, whereas Schnell's score stood at 94 when he was killed on 25 February 1944 while serving with JG 54 on the Eastern Front.

## JG 1 in action

JG 1's main operational area was along the Dutch coast and its first Fw 190s were taken on by *Hauptmann* Hans von Hahn's II *Gruppe* based at Woensdrecht. By July 1942 all three *Gruppen* plus 10 *Staffeln* had been re-equipped, total strength amounting to 127 aircraft. Over the coming months JG 1 would be kept extremely busy dealing with RAF Circus and Ramrod operations against targets in Holland and Belgium, and Roadstead operations aimed at disrupting shipping on its way to Rotterdam.

JG 1 was also the first line of defence against daylight attacks by Eighth Air Force heavy bombers. Over the coming months it was to include a number of aces within its ranks including *Major* Heinz Bar who was to command II *Gruppe* and finish the war with 220 kills. In April 1943 the *Geschwader* helped create JG 11 when its I *Gruppe* (Bf 109) and III *Gruppe* (Fw 190) were transferred to the new unit which was tasked with Reich defence.

Towards the end of 1942 the 'happy' time for the *Kanalgeschwader* was beginning to come to an end, as attacks by medium and heavy bombers were gradually being stepped up and the much-improved Spitfire IX was appearing in ever increasing numbers. The *Jagdwaffe*, however, had the benefit of a highly skilled ground control organisation which (usually) ensured that it had tactical advantage. This, together with the lack of a true long-range escort fighter on the Allied side, meant that the top *Luftwaffe* pilots could still accumulate big scores. One of JG 26's most successful pilots from this period was *Oberleutnant* Wilhelm-Ferdinand 'Wutz' Galland.

The third Galland brother to fly with JG 26, 'Wutz' had arrived in June 1941 and had already been decorated for his service in a flak

In contrast to the previous picture, this Fw 190A-4/U8 has its 300-litre drop tanks mounted on streamlined Junkers fairings. Contrary to expectations, they produced more drag than unfaired mounts.

regiment prior to becoming a pilot. He was given command of the 5th *Staffel* in June 1942 and took over II *Gruppe* in January 1943. By this time his score stood at 21, a figure that was to increase steadily in the coming months. One of Galland's most successful days occurred on 4 April 1943 when he claimed two B-17s that had been raiding the Renault factory near Paris, and an escorting Spitfire IX. In conjunction with I./JG 2, led by Walter Oesau, Galland's pilots went for the bombers head on, ensuring that the spacing of each *Schwarm* was sufficiently close so that succeeding sections could catch any aircraft that had been forced out of position. Despite the better performance of the Spitfire IX, the three RAF escort squadrons lost seven aircraft, of which five fell to JG 26 and two to JG 2.

Galland was to meet his death on 17 August 1943 during the infamous Eighth Air Force raid on Schweinfurt. II./JG 26 was directed to attack the bombers on their return and took off from Lille-Nord in the late afternoon, meeting up with the bomber stream near the German/Belgian border. Unknown to them,

Colonel 'Hub' Zemke's 56th Fighter Group had set out to escort the bombers home and instead of dropping their overload tanks on crossing the enemy coast (as was the usual practice) had retained them for an extra ten minutes which had allowed them to fly fifteen miles into German territory, farther than they had ever been before. Galland led his pilots in a head-on attack on the bombers but they were quickly engulfed by Zemke's P-47s which appeared from the south-east, an entirely unexpected direction. Despite frantic warnings by his wingman, *Unteroffizier* Heinz Gomann, Galland was shot down and killed. Gomann was also shot down but survived and ended the war with twelve kills to his name.

## 190 spreads its wings

By the latter half of 1942, the Fw 190 was beginning to spread its wings over all areas of the European conflict. As the RAF were dependent on the Spitfire Vc and P-40 in the Mediterranean theatre of operations, the arrival of *Oberleutnant* Adolf Dickfeld's II./JG 2 in Tunisia in November had a similar effect to the

A well known view of *Oberleutnant* Armin Faber's Fw 190A-3 parked at Pembrey in June 1942. Faber offered to fly the 190 in mock combat with Spitfires with minimal fuel, but it was obvious to everyone that he would take to his parachute at the earliest opportunity and his kind offer was declined.

A close-up view of an Fw 190A-3 during a break from manufacturer's trials. This aircraft retains the design armament of MG 17 machine-guns in the wing roots, although the normal wing-mounted armament in service comprised two MG 151/20 cannon with the option of two MG FF cannon outboard. Note the underwing blister to accommodate the ammunition drum of the MG FF cannon.

The standard Fw 190 armament seen in the top photograph needed upgrading to deal with the threat of USAAF heavy bombers. This Fw 190A-5/U11 was one of the development aircraft for the A-8/R3 heavy fighter. Armament consisted of two engine-mounted MG 17s, two wing root MG 151/20s and two pod-mounted 30-mm MK 103 cannon. Although possessing a heavy weight of fire, the MK 103 was not particularly accurate and imposed penalties in terms of weight and drag that limited its use.

Fw 190A-5/U12 *Werke* Nr 813 BH+CC was one of two development aircraft for the under-wing WB 151 weapons container which accommodated two MG 151/20 cannon. Six 20-mm cannon amounted to a hefty punch, but performance was again reduced substantially owing to weight and drag. Nevertheless, this weapons fit saw limited operational use commencing with the A-6/R1 model of the Fw 190.

190's first appearance over northern France a year before. Although the unit was only active in this area for four months, it managed to destroy over 150 Allied aircraft, the majority falling to Dickfeld, *Oberleutnant* Kurt Buhlingen, leader of the 4th *Staffel* and *Leutnant* Erich Rudorffer of the 6th *Staffel*.

## Retreat from Africa

Having been based initially at Bizerta and Tingja-South, II./JG 2 moved to Kairouan in early January 1943, and it was here on 8 January that Dickfeld was injured in a take-off accident. On recovery he was to lead II./JG 11 before being given a staff appointment. In the meantime his two *Staffelkapitän*s continued to set an example, and by the time the *Gruppe* returned to north-west France in March 1943, Buhlingen's score in the Mediterranean had risen to 40 with Rudorffer not far behind with 27. By the end of the war Buhlingen had achieved

his century with 112 kills, while Rudorffer went on to be the seventh highest scoring *Luftwaffe* ace with 222 victories, a figure that includes 124 kills with JG 54 on the Eastern Front.

At the other end of Europe the Fw 190A-3s of I and IV./JG 5 had a relatively leisurely existence as they guarded the Norwegian coast from incursions by RAF Mosquitos. Although aerial activity was minimal, the setting up of a *Jabo Staffel* in February 1943 (14./JG 5 under *Hauptmann* Friedrich-Wilhelm Strakeljahn) had spectacular success against shipping in the Arctic. By the end of the year vessels with a combined gross of 39,000 tons had been sunk.

Although successful, the use of the Fw 190 as a makeshift night-fighter in the latter half of 1943 had led to an ever-increasing accident rate. The eventual recovery of the twin-engined Bf 110 and Ju 88 units, following the difficulties caused by the use of 'Window', allowed the experiment to be quickly concluded. Even so,

Fw 190A-3/U3 *Werke Nr 447* carries four SC 50 bombs on an ER 4 rack attached to a standard ETC 501 rack. This arrangement was a common sight on the Fw 190F and G ground-attack variants of the fighter.

some pilots achieved success, including *Oberleutnant* Kurt Welter and *Major* Friedrich-Karl Muller of JG 300 who ultimately achieved 56 and 30 night kills respectively. Muller was the leading *Wilde Sau Experte* with 23 victories.

## On the Eastern Front

While pressure was gradually being increased in the west, in the Mediterranean, and in the skies over Germany by day and night, some of the most serious setbacks for the Reich were occurring many hundreds of miles away to the east. Despite the fact that the Fw 190 was more suited to operations in the Russian theatre than the Bf 109, it was not to be used in any great number, and even at its peak there were rarely more than 200 machines available to cover a front line extending over 1,000 miles. The hazards of operating in this area were highlighted by the fate of *Hauptmann* Heinrich Krafft, *Kommodore* of I./JG 51, a 78-kill ace, who died in Russian hands after being shot down by

flak on 14 December 1942. His successor, *Oberstleutnant* Karl-Gottfried Nordmann, was then injured in a mid-air collision with his wingman so that I *Gruppe* was taken over by *Major* Erich Leie who quickly began to add to the 43 victories he had achieved with JG 2. His total eventually rose to 118 before he was killed in 1945 when flying as leader of JG 77.

If a pilot was fortunate enough to survive the murderous Russian flak and had sufficient ability to deal with fighters, the opportunities to compile high scores were better in the east than anywhere else. One of the rising stars of I./JG 51 was *Oberleutnant* Joachim Brendal who was eventually credited with 189 victories.

By December 1942 III./JG 51 had converted to the Fw 190A-4 and numbered within its ranks another *Experte*, *Oberleutnant* Gunther Schack of the 9th *Staffel*. Schack was extremely aggressive in the air and his ability as a marksman meant that he was particularly adept at deflection shooting. On at least two

This Fw 190F-2 shows SG 4's emblem of an axe-wielding mouse riding on a bomb, with a tropical filter beneath the badge. As in the previous picture, the fighter is also fitted with an ER 4 rack on an ETC 501.

occasions he was to claim five kills in a single sortie, his final victory tally being 174.

Another mainstay of the fighter force on the Russian front was JG 54, led by *Oberstleutnant* Hannes Trautloft. JG 54 began to convert to the Fw 190A-4 in December 1942, and was to produce four pilots who all scored over 200 victories. First to reach this mark was *Hauptmann* Hans Philipp, *Kommodore* of I *Gruppe* who achieved his 200th kill on 17 March 1943. Not long after he was given command of JG 1, but on 8 October 1943 was shot down and killed by a P-47, by which time his score had risen to 206. Next in the list of JG 54's top scorers was *Major* Erich Rudorffer

whose final total of 222 kills included 86 over northern France and the Mediterranean and 12 jet kills secured late in the war in the Messerschmitt Me 262 as leader of II./JG 7.

## Walter Nowotny

Perhaps the most famous of them all, *Major* Walter Nowotny's long combat career had begun in July 1941 and he already had 50 victories to his name by the time he came to fly the new Focke-Wulf fighter. His exploits with the Fw 190 were legendary and rapid promotion to become leader of I./JG 54 resulted. Nowotny was another who chalked up multiple kills, on one occasion shooting

By 1943, increasingly heavy raids by the US Eighth Air Force led to the development of weapons capable of being fired from outside an American bomber's field of fire. These included WGr 21 rockets, mounted under the wings of this Fw 190A-4/R6. Although extremely effective against bombers flying in close formation, problems were experienced with accuracy and assessment of range.

down seven Soviet fighters in one sortie. Three more victories were to follow in the afternoon making it ten in one day. Nowotny's 250th kill was recorded on 14 October 1943. He was to leave I./JG 54 in February 1944 and was killed on 8 November when his Me 262 crashed at Achmer after combat with P-51s. His total of 258 victories made him Germany's fifth highest scoring ace.

## 190 top scorer

The top scoring Fw 190 ace was *Oberleutnant* Otto Kittel, who had joined JG 54 as a *Feldwebel* (Sergeant) in 1941. After making a slow start, his score began to rise rapidly after he converted to the 190 and by the time of his death on 14 February 1945 his tally stood at 267. That was enough to make him the fourth highest scoring ace of all time.

With the failure of the German offensive at Kursk in the summer of 1943, the hard-pressed pilots of JG 51 and 54 had to fight like never before, especially as the defeat was rapidly

followed by a Russian counter-offensive. Many high scoring aces were lost around this time, including *Major* Rudolf Resch, the commander of IV./JG 51, who was killed on 11 July having accumulated 96 kills. Two weeks later the popular *Leutnant* Josef 'Pepi' Jennewein of I./JG 51 was lost, most of his 86 kills having been gained on the Fw 190. JG 54 also suffered the loss of experienced pilots including several *Staffel* leaders. *Hauptmann* Heinrich Jung, *Kapitän* of the 4th *Staffel*, a victor in 68 aerial combats, was shot down and killed by Russian fighters on 30 July, and the 2nd *Staffel's Hauptmann* Hans Gotz (82 kills) died as a result of return fire from Ilyushin Il-2 *Shturmoviks* on 4 August. Not long afterwards the 5th *Staffel* lost its leader when *Hauptmann* Max Stotz (189 kills) was posted missing after baling out over enemy territory on 19 August.

## Soviet advances

After Kursk the initiative was firmly seized by the Russians. For the two remaining Fw 190

A gun camera view of an Fw 190 of JG 2 coming under attack from a Hawker Typhoon flown by Flight Sergeant Derek Erasmus of 266 Squadron. The Typhoons were taking part in a Circus operation near Guipavas on 15 August 1943, and lost three aircraft including that of Squadron Leader A.S. McIntyre.

*Gruppen* of JG 51 (*Major* Erich Leie's I *Gruppe* and *Hauptmann* Fritz Losigkeit's III *Gruppe* – IV *Gruppe* having reverted to the Bf 109) the stress of almost constant combat was now mixed with frequent moves in the face of Russian advances. Increasing loss rates because of enemy action, accidents and the destruction of aircraft to prevent them falling into Russian hands, led to problems with the supply of replacement machines. By early 1944 JG 51 (with the exception of the *Stabsstaffel*) had been re-equipped with the Bf 109G.

However, I and II./JG 54 were to retain their Fw 190s for the remainder of the war and were to be part of the increasingly desperate rearguard actions trying to stem Russian progress towards the German border.

Although none of JG 54's pilots were to match the likes of Nowotny and Kittel in the last eighteen months of the war, some were to come close, in particular *Leutnant* Emil Lang of the 5th *Staffel*. A former pilot with Lufthansa, Lang shot to prominence in late October 1943 when he destroyed an incredible 18 aircraft in one day, a feat that placed him firmly in the record books.

Lang was to go on to claim 173 kills, the last 14 of which were recorded in the west as the leader of II./JG 26. He was killed on 3 September 1944 when his Fw 190A-8 was shot down by an Allied fighter near Brussels, most probably by a P-51 of the 55th Fighter Group, although Spitfire XIIs of 41 Squadron were also in the area.

An Fw 190F-9 fighter-bomber captured by US forces at the end of the war. This ground-attack variant of the Fw 190 is fitted with four ETC 50 racks under the wings, each capable of carrying a 50-kg (110-lb) SC 50 bomb.

Another high scoring ace from this period was the 6th *Staffel's Oberleutnant* Albin Wolf who had the honour of recording JG 54's 7,000th victory on 23 March 1944. Just ten days later Wolf was killed when his aircraft was hit by flak, his score at the time standing at 144.

By the summer of 1944 I and II./JG 54 were operating from bases in the Courland peninsula in Latvia, where they would remain for the rest of the war despite numerous Russian attempts to eliminate German forces in the area. Further losses were sustained including that of *Major* Horst Ademeit (166 kills), leader of I *Gruppe*, who fell to light flak on 8 August. His replacement was another high scoring ace, *Major* Franz Eisenach who was eventually credited with 129 victories.

Yet another milestone was passed on 15 October 1944 when *Oberleutnant* Helmut Wettstein, *Kapitän* of the 6th *Staffel*, claimed JG 54's 8,000th victory, but experienced pilots continued to be lost including the 1st *Staffel's Leutnant* Heinz Wernicke (117 kills) who collided with his wingman on 27 December when in combat near Riga. The most serious setback, however, occurred on 14 February 1945 when Otto Kittel finally fell to defensive fire from a formation of Il-2 *Shturmoviks*. I and II./JG 54 were to hold out to the very end and the eventual evacuation saw the Fw 190 take on a transport role as operational equipment was removed to reduce weight and ground personnel crammed into every available space for the flight back to the west. The radio compartment behind the cockpit and the rear fuselage were commonly used: less obvious

One of the aircraft used to develop the Fw 190 G-series is fitted with an ETC 501 rack under the fuselage and an ETC 503 rack under each wing. It also has a wingtip-mounted pitot tube, as used on the G-8, and a tropical filter, but retains engine-mounted MG 131 machine-guns normally deleted on G-series aircraft.

was the ammunition bay in each wing, which could accommodate one (small) person.

In the meantime, the much improved Fw 190D-9 had entered service with III./JG 54 in September 1944, followed before the end of the year by I and II./JG 26 and III./JG 2. The Third *Gruppe* of JG 54 had been withdrawn from the Eastern front in January 1943, swapping places with *Major* Johannes Seifert's I./JG 26, but unlike the latter, it did not return to its original theatre of operations. The association between III./JG 54 and JG 26 was close and was epitomised by its leader *Hauptmann* Robert Weiss, who had flown with 6./JG 26 in 1941/42. In recognition of this relationship III./JG 54 was put under the command of the *Schlageter Geschwader* and was to become IV./JG 26 on 25 February 1945. Weiss did not live to see this day, however, as he was shot down and killed by Spitfires of 331 Squadron on 29 December 1944. His final tally stood at 121.

## *Sturmgruppen* in action

The success achieved by *Sturmstaffel* 1 had encouraged the setting up of three *Sturmgruppen* (IV./JG 3, II./JG 300 and II./JG 4) in an attempt to slow the American bomber offensive on the Reich that had been resumed following the successful landings in Normandy. The destruction of a four-engined heavy bomber was the most prized victory of all, and several pilots were to have the necessary skill and nerve to accumulate high scores in this particular category.

Topping the list was *Major* Walther Dahl of JGs 3 and 300 who counted 36 bombers out of a total of 128 kills. This figure was matched by *Major* Georg-Peter Eder. All but 10 of his wartime total of 78 victories were achieved in the west with JGs 1, 2 and 26. Ranking third in the list of bomber destroyers was *Major* Anton 'Toni' Hackl, also ex-JG 26, with 32 four-engined heavies among his 192 kills.

The *Luftwaffe* fighter force was ruined by the disastrous Operation *Bodenplatte* which took place on 1 January 1945. Allied bases in Holland and Belgium were hit hard in an early morning strike, but while Allied aircraft were replaced within days, the loss of some of the *Jagdwaffe*'s most experienced pilots could not be made good. The remaining Fw 190-equipped units struggled on in the face of opposition that enjoyed an ever-increasing numerical advantage. This situation was made worse by constant upheavals, as bases had to be given up, and by a chronic lack of fuel caused by strategic Allied attacks on key oil refineries and constant disruption of transport.

## The ultimate 190 in action

One of the few bright spots in the final months of the war was the delivery in early March 1945 of the first Ta 152H-1s to the *Stabsschwarm* of JG 301 under *Oberstleutnant* Fritz Aufhammer. The Ta 152 was used to provide cover for the Fw 190D-9s of I and II./JG 301 as they carried out their duties, and also for airfield protection as marauding Allied fighters liked nothing better than to find the opposition with its gear down and ready for landing. So late was its introduction to service, however, that only nine aircraft were claimed as destroyed before the war ended, five being credited to *Oberfeldwebel* Josef Keil and three to *Oberfeldwebel* Willi Reschke.

## Jet defenders

Airfield defence duties were also undertaken by a small *Staffel* of Fw 190D-9s attached to *Jagdverband* (JV) 44, the Me 262 unit set up by *General* Adolf Galland that operated out of Munich-Riem in the last few weeks of the war. This *Platzschutzstaffel* (airfield protection unit) was led by *Leutnant* Heinz Sachsenberg, an ace with 104 victories achieved during service with JG 52. Other pilots known to have flown with the unit are *Hauptmann* Waldemar Wubke, *Oberleutnant* Klaus Faber, *Leutnant* Karl-Heinz Hofmann and *Feldwebel* Bodo Dirschauer. The D-9s flown by JV 44 featured the most flamboyant colour scheme of any Fw 190 unit as the undersides were overall red with white longitudinal stripes. This was applied so that the aircraft could be easily identified by

Apart from a shattered windscreen, missing hood and cowling panel, this Fw 190A-8 abandoned at Melsbroek is virtually complete. Note the raised access panel for the wing root MG 151/20 cannon and open fuel filler flap just above it.

German anti-aircraft gunners, the need for such a striking scheme hinting at the large numbers of Allied fighters that were in the skies over the Reich at that time. The unit badge was a black and white checkerboard in a red circle, and each aircraft carried an individual inscription below the cockpit. That for Sachsenberg's Red 1 (*Werke* Nr 600424) was written in a southern dialect, and it read '*Verkaufts mei Gwand, Ich foahrs in Himmeil*' which translates as 'Sell my kit, I'm going to Heaven'.

# 4. Accomplishments: Flying the Fw 190

The word 'classic' is much abused at times. Occasionally it can be seen attached to a product of the automotive or aeronautical industry whose only real achievement is in reaching a certain age – but that it applies to the Focke-Wulf Fw 190 there can be no doubt. From the moment of its first flight it was clear that the Fw 190 would be capable of performance liable to make most other fighters obsolescent, a promise that was realised when it entered service two years later. Over the next twelve months the combat reports of many RAF fighter pilots gave assessments (often contradictory) of the Fw 190's abilities, and its performance in comparison with the Spitfire V was the main reason for an alarming increase in the amount of 'twitch' being generated in Fighter Command squadrons.

Although no design can ever achieve perfection, the Fw 190 got as close as any. It mated the most powerful engine that was available to a small, compact airframe of low wetted area to keep drag to a minimum, whilst at the same time combining great strength with low structural weight. In addition to ensuring ease of manufacture and maintenance, every aspect of its design was carefully analysed to provide the pilot with a machine that made his task as easy as possible. The wide-track undercarriage greatly improved ground stability in comparison with the Bf 109, and the large frameless canopy allowed vastly superior all-round vision, a factor that was to save many pilots' lives as it was far easier to see hostile aircraft before they could get within range.

As a fighter, it had to be able to manoeuvre rapidly, particularly in the rolling plane, and the Fw 190 was to appear with a wing planform and ailerons that would not disgrace an aerobatic monoplane of today. The ailerons were particularly large so that rolling manoeuvres could be initiated which very few fighters could follow. The fact that they were operated by push/pull rods instead of the more conventional wires and pulleys meant that the controls felt more precise, and there was less chance of control response deteriorating owing to the high loadings imposed during combat. The other control surfaces were heavier to operate, although not excessively so. The fact that out-of-trim forces caused by attitude changes were few, and there was no tendency to yaw when applying bank, meant that control inputs in pitch and yaw were less than in many other agile aircraft.

## Powerful engine

Another prime requirement for a fighter is high speed, and this came courtesy of the BMW 801 14-cylinder radial of 1,600 hp. At a time when the most powerful in-line engines in service, the Daimler-Benz DB 601 and Rolls-Royce Merlin III, were producing a little over 1,000 hp, the BMW 801 offered power in abundance and Fw 190 pilots had the luxury of being able to fight as and when they chose. They could also employ the aircraft's excellent acceleration and dive performance to disengage at will. The power available even allowed pilots the opportunity to make up for the turn rate, one of

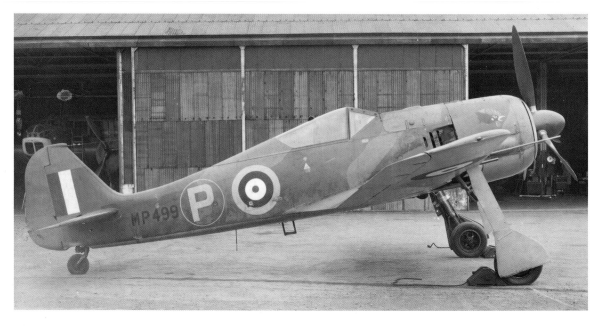

After *Oberleutnant* Armin Faber presented his Fw 190A-3 to the RAF at Pembrey on 23 June 1942, it was given the serial number MP499 and evaluated by RAE. Despite the application of standard camouflage colours it retains JG 2's cock's head motif on the engine cowling. This insignia originated with JG 2's *Kommodore* Hans 'Assi' Hahn, whose surname is the German for cockerel.

the Fw 190's few shortcomings: for example they could select 15 degrees of flap to tighten the rate of turn, increasing power to overcome the increase in drag and maintain speed. The air-cooled radial also offered peace of mind in that it could withstand quite serious battle damage and often keep going sufficiently long to get a pilot home, in some cases with one or two cylinder heads shot away.

By the summer of 1942 the level of dominance that the Fw 190 had achieved over the Spitfire V led some in the British military hierarchy to seriously consider acquiring an example by clandestine means. A seemingly outlandish scheme formulated by Captain Philip Pinckney, a Commando officer, involved stealing an Fw 190 from a *Luftwaffe* airfield in northern France, but happily for all involved (not least for test pilot Jeffrey Quill, who had been 'volunteered' to fly it), the issue was resolved by the sudden, well documented arrival of *Oberleutnant* Armin Faber in his Fw 190A-3 at Pembrey on 23 June 1942.

The subsequent testing of Faber's machine showed just how good the Fw 190 was,

although it also went some way to dispel certain stories that had begun to circulate within Fighter Command squadrons.

A letter dated 27 July 1942 from the Under Secretary of State for Air, Captain Harold Balfour, to Air Marshal Sholto Douglas hints at the aura that had become attached to the 190. In it, he expressed the view that it would be a good idea to demonstrate it at selected fighter airfields within 10, 11 and 12 Groups so that pilots could see it 'in the flesh'. They would then realise that it was 'not a mythical super aeroplane, but simply a very fine aircraft with advantages which must be watched carefully and some disadvantages from which benefit can be derived...' Before that could take place, a full trial was carried out at the Air Fighting Development Unit at Duxford. The qualities of the Fw 190 were described as follows:

## Flying characteristics

'The aircraft is pleasant to fly, all controls being extremely light and positive. The aircraft is difficult to taxi due to excessive weight on the self-centring tailwheel when on the ground. For

The head on view of MP499 clearly displays the exceptionally clean lines of the Fw 190 and its tightly cowled BMW 801 radial engine. Note the Hotspur glider to the left of picture.

take-off, 15 degrees of flap is required and it is necessary to keep the control column back to avoid swinging during the initial stage of the take off run. The run is approximately the same as that of the Spitfire IX.

'Once airborne the pilot immediately feels at home in the aircraft. The retraction of the flaps and undercarriage is barely noticeable although the aircraft will sink if the retraction of the flaps is made before a reasonably high airspeed has been obtained.

'The stalling speed of the aircraft is high, being approximately 110 mph with undercarriage and flaps retracted and 105 mph with undercarriage and flaps fully down. All controls are effective up to the stall.

The rear view of the Fw 190 was one that very few Spitfire V pilots got to see in 1941 and 1942. The distinctive splay of the main undercarriage legs and the large ailerons are readily apparent.

Another aspect of MP499 that emphasizes the pugnacious character of the Fw 190. Although some pilots preferred to have the outer MG FF cannon removed to reduce weight and increase performance, they are retained on Faber's aircraft. With its BMW 801D-2 engine the A-3 had cooling slots as standard

'One excellent feature of this aircraft is that it is seldom necessary to re-trim under all conditions of flight.

'The best approach speed for landing with flaps and undercarriage down is between 130 and 140 mph indicated, reducing to about 125 mph when crossing the edge of the aerodrome. Owing to the steep angle of glide, the view during the approach is good and the actual landing is straightforward, the touchdown occurring at approximately 110 mph. The landing run is about the same as the Spitfire IX. The locking of the tailwheel again assists in preventing swing during the landing run.

'The aircraft is very pleasant for aerobatics, even at high speed.

## Performance

'The all-round performance of the Fw 190 is good. Only brief performance tests have been carried out and the figures obtained give a maximum speed of approximately 390 mph True, 1.42 ata (atmospheres) boost, 2,700 rpm at the maximum power altitude of about 18,000 ft. All flights at maximum power were carried out

for a duration of 2 minutes only.

'There are indications that the engine of this aircraft is de-rated, this being supported by the pilot's instruction card found in the cockpit and by information obtained from PoWs. Further performance tests and engine investigation are to be carried out by the RAE and more definite information will then be available.

'Throughout the trials the engine has been running very roughly and as a result pilots flying the aircraft have had little confidence in its reliability. The cause of the roughness has not yet been ascertained, but it is thought that it may be due to a bad period of vibration at certain engine speeds which may also affect the injection system. It is understood from PoWs who have flown the aircraft that the roughness of the engine is usual and that they also have little faith in its reliability, in fact they dislike flying the Fw 190 over the sea.

## Endurance

'The total of 115 gallons of fuel is carried in two self-sealing tanks and each tank is fitted with an immersed fuel pump for use at altitude. A total of 9 gallons of oil is carried in a protected oil tank. The approximate endurance under operational condition, including dogfights and a climb to 25,000 ft, is approximately 1 hour 20 minutes. There is a red warning light fitted in a prominent position which illuminates when there is only sufficient fuel left for 20 minutes of flying remaining.

## Climb

'The rate of climb up to 18,000 ft under maximum continuous climbing conditions at 1.35 ata boost, 2,450 rpm, 165 mph is between 3,000 to 3,250 ft/min. The initial rate of climb when pulling up from level flight at fast cruising speed is high and the angle steep and from a dive is phenomenal. It is considered that the de-rated version of the Fw 190 is unlikely to be met above 25,000 ft as the power of the engine starts falling off at 22,000 ft and by 25,000 ft has fallen off considerably. It is not possible to give the rate of climb at this altitude.

## Dive

'The Fw 190 has a high rate of dive, the initial acceleration being excellent. The maximum speed so far obtained in a dive is 580 mph True at 16,000 ft and at this speed the controls, although slightly heavier, are still remarkably light. One very good feature is that no alteration of trim from level flight is required either during the entry or during the pull-out. Due to the injection system it is possible to enter the dive by pushing the control column forward without the engine cutting. *[Note: interrogation of Focke-Wulf personnel after the war revealed that the Fw 190 had been dived to Mach 0.80, a marked nose down trim change occurring at*

Close-up of the hood on Faber's Fw 190A-3 at Pembrey. Of note are the heavily raked windscreen and the roller assembly for the radio antenna. The armoured headrest is of the earlier narrow type with a single support.

Ease of access to the BMW 801D-2 and MG 17 machine-guns is apparent in this view of MP499. Background detail has been obliterated by the wartime censor (compare with photo on page 63).

*Mach 0.78 for which the variable incidence tailplane was extremely useful in assisting recovery.]*

## Search view

'The view for search from the Fw 190 is the best that has yet been seen by this Unit. The cockpit hood is of moulded Plexiglas and offers an unrestricted view all round. No rear view mirror is fitted and it is considered unnecessary as the backward view is so good. The hood must not be opened in flight as it is understood that tail buffeting may occur and that there is a chance of the hood being blown off. This, however, is not a disadvantage for day search as the quality of the Plexiglas is excellent. During conditions of bad visibility and rain, or in the event of oil being thrown on the windscreen, the fact that the hood must not be opened is obviously a disadvantage.

'The aircraft, although extremely light on all controls, is reasonably easy to fly on instruments. There are no artificial horizon or climb and dive indicators, which are naturally missed by English pilots. It appears that instrument flying is carried out by use of the gyro compass, turn and bank indicator, altimeter and airspeed indicator.

## Low flying

'The good all-round view from the aircraft, particularly over the nose, makes the Fw 190 very suitable for low flying and ground strafing. Another good point is that the sight is depressed which would probably help in preventing pilots from flying into the ground. In conditions of bad visibility however, low flying is likely to be unpleasant as the hood must not be opened in flight.

## Formation flying

'The aircraft is easy to fly in formation and due to the good view, all types of formation can be

The cockpit interior of the Fw 190A-3 was years ahead of its time and offered a neat, well laid out display well before the term ergonomics had even been thought of. The coaming is surmounted by the Revi 12C/D gunsight with the round counters below and to the left. The six main instruments below are (left to right) altimeter, ASI, turn and slip, compass, boost gauge and rpm gauge. The four smaller dials below these are fuel and oil pressure gauge, oil temperature, fuel contents and propeller pitch indicator. The centre panel contains the bomb release control. Notable omissions are an artificial horizon and vertical speed indicator

flown without difficulty. The aircraft has a wide speed range which greatly assists in regaining formation, but care must be taken to avoid over-shooting, as its clean lines make deceleration slow.

## Night flying

'The aircraft was not flown at night but was inspected with the engine running on a dark night, with no moon. The cockpit lighting appeared very efficient and did not reflect on the canopy. The exhaust flames viewed from about 100 yards ahead were seen as a dull red halo and viewed from the beam could be seen from about 500 yards away. The flame can be seen from astern about 200 yards away. It is considered that the glare will badly affect the pilot, particularly during take-off and landing. Although the aircraft carried full night flying equipment, there is no indication that flame dampers are normally fitted. It is possible that

the cause of the red flame may be due to the use of a faulty fuel mixture.

## Conclusions

'The Fw 190 is undoubtedly a formidable low and medium altitude fighter. Its designer has obviously given much thought to the pilot. The cockpit is extremely well laid out and the absence of large levers and unnecessary gadgets is most noticeable. The pilot is given a comfortable seating position and is well protected by armour. The simplicity of the aircraft as a whole is an excellent feature and enables new pilots to be thoroughly conversant with all controls in a very brief period. The rough running of the engine is much disliked by all pilots and must be a great disadvantage as lack of confidence in an engine makes flying over bad country or water most unpleasant.

'The armament is good and well positioned and the ammunition capacity should be sufficient for any normal fighter operation. The sighting view is approximately half a ring better than that from the Spitfire. The all-round search view is the best that has yet been seen from any aircraft flown by this Unit. The flying characteristics are exceptional and a pilot new to the type feels at home within the first few minutes of flight. The controls are light and well harmonised and all manoeuvres can be carried out without difficulty at all speeds. The fact that the Fw 190 does not require re-trimming under all conditions of flight is a particularly good point.

'The initial acceleration is very good and is particularly noticeable in the initial stages of a climb or dive. Perhaps one of the most outstanding qualities of this aircraft is the remarkable aileron control. It is possible to change from a turn in one direction to a turn in the opposite direction with incredible speed and when viewed from another aircraft the change appears just as if a flick half roll had been made. It is considered that night flying would be unpleasant, particularly for landing and take off due to the exhaust glare and the fact that the cockpit canopy cannot be opened in flight. The engine is easy to start but requires running up for a considerable time, even when warm, before the oil temperature reaches the safety margin for take-off and this coupled with the fact that the aircraft is not easy to taxi, makes the Fw 190 inferior to our aircraft for quick take-offs.

## Comparison with rivals

'The comparative fighting qualities of the Fw 190 have been compared with a Spitfire Vb, Spitfire IX, Mustang Ia, P-38F, 4-cannon Typhoon and a prototype Griffon Spitfire, all aircraft being flown by experienced pilots. The main conclusion gained from the tactical trials of the Fw 190 is that our fighter aircraft must fly at high speed when in an area where the Fw 190 is likely to be met. This will give our pilots the chance of bouncing and catching the Fw 190, and if bounced themselves, the best chance of avoiding being shot down. The all-round search view from the Fw 190 being exceptional makes it rather difficult to achieve the element of surprise. Here again, however, the advantage of our aircraft flying at high speed must not be overlooked as they may, even if seen by the pilot of the Fw 190, catch it before it has time to dive away.'

By the summer of 1943 the supply of Fw 190s available to the British had improved considerably, courtesy of the nocturnal activities of SKG 10 who were tasked with carrying out attacks against targets in the UK. On the night of 16/17 April 1943 no fewer than three Fw 190s arrived at West Malling following an attack on London. *Oberfeldwebel* Otto Schultz crashed A-4/U-8 *Werke* Nr 7152 on the approach, *Oberleutnant* Fritz Setzer landed A-5/U-8 *Werke* Nr 2719 on fire (it subsequently exploded), and *Feldwebel* Otto Bechtold landed A-4/U-8 Werke Nr 7155. Bechtold's machine

was the only one of the three that could be used, but two more Fw 190s were acquired soon after when SKG 10 pilots landed in error at Manston on 20 May and 20 June 1943. The first to arrive was *Unteroffizier* Heinz Ehrhardt in A-4/U-8 *Werke* Nr 5843, which became PN999 and was used by the RAE before being sent to 1426 (Enemy Aircraft) Flight on 28 September 1943.

During its time at the RAE, PN999 was flown by Squadron Leader Johnny Checketts, DFC who at the time was OC 485 (New Zealand) Squadron at Biggin Hill. His impressions of the Fw 190 were given in a letter to 11 Group HQ dated 27 August 1943:

## One pilot's impressions

'This flight was made by me to find the differences in the Fw 190 and the Spitfire IX (Merlin 66) aircraft in regard to flying qualities. The Fw 190 number PN999 which I flew was not taken higher than 4,000 ft so that the experience I gained was very limited in the 30 minutes I flew.

'I found the cockpit and controls extremely well laid out and that every switch and all the flying controls were very convenient and easy to work. Starting was remarkably simple, and with more experience on the aircraft, I should imagine that scramble time would compare with Spitfires. Taxying is reasonably easy but the toe brakes are strange after hand brake control and I think that the Spitfire is much better for taxying.

## Take-off and flight

'The take-off was terrifying and I had considerable difficulty in keeping the aircraft straight in spite of the fact that I held the stick back to lock the tail wheel. I think I opened the throttle too slowly because I saw the same aircraft take off before I flew it in a perfectly normal manner. The electrical undercarriage is very simply raised and the tail trim is quite effective. The machine is beautiful to fly and quite fast at normal cruising revs and boost which I did not exceed. I had been warned about an extremely rough engine but under cruising conditions I found that the engine behaved perfectly and compared with most radials. When I was about eight miles south of

MP499 taking off with 15 degrees of flap set, elevator trim at neutral and propeller pitch to AUTO. At 2,700 rpm and 23.5 lb (1.6 ata) boost the take-off run was similar to that of the Spitfire IX and the Fw 190 lifted off at around 112 mph. There was some tendency to swing to port due to propeller torque but this could easily be held with the application of right rudder.

base two Mustangs saw me and made attacks, dummy or real I don't know, I did not give these aircraft any chance but owing to their insistence I let them see my RAF markings and they formated on me and then tried to play. In the resulting steep turns at maximum cruising boost and revs I found no difficulty in getting on the tail of these aircraft and could have easily shot them down. I found the Revi gunsight very pleasant to use and the gun buttons in a comfortable position on the control column. The rate of climb of the Fw 190 was greatly superior to the Mustangs but inferior to the Spitfire IX (Merlin 66). I should imagine that at lower than 22,000 ft the Fw 190 would be slightly better than the Spitfire IX (Merlin 61).

'When the Mustangs sheered off I tried rolls and general defensive flying. The Fw 190 is remarkable and really beautiful to aerobat in the rolling plane but in the looping plane it is greatly inferior to the Spitfire. Visibility is exceptionally good all round and is greatly superior to the Spitfire. I found the cockpit slightly small for defensive fighting and the back parachute was uncomfortable, which might account for the fact that attacks on the Fw 190 from below and behind often catch the Fw pilot unawares.

## Landing and overshoot

'On my first approach I found the vital actions easy and comfortable, although landing with the hood closed was strange. I was forced round again by a Spitfire cutting in and the overshoot procedure was normal and the aircraft behaved perfectly. On my second approach I came in at 130 mph and used motor; the landing position is very blind and uncomfortable, but if the aircraft is motored in at 120–130 mph a three-point landing is easily made although swing after landing is noticeable. I enjoyed the experience and should like to fly this aircraft at 22,000 ft to 30,000 ft to gain experience at its combat heights. I am convinced through experience that the Spitfire with the Merlin 66 engine is much superior at all levels, but the Fw 190 could be a very aggressive aircraft in the hands of an experienced fighter pilot.'

In addition to testing of the Fw 190A in the UK, the USAAF carried out trials in Italy in

December 1943 using a captured example against a Republic P-47D-4 Thunderbolt. Both carried a typical combat load and the tests were flown from sea level up to 10,000 ft. The Fw 190 was considered to be in exceptionally good condition for a captured machine and achieved 42 in of boost pressure on take-off, although it lacked the P-47D's water injection.

During acceleration tests the Fw 190 initially held an advantage at all heights and speeds, quickly gaining about 200 yards, but at 330 mph IAS (Indicated Air Speed) the P-47 began to overtake rapidly and quickly drew away. The story was very much the same in the climb with the Fw 190 being superior over the first 1,500 ft, but thereafter the P-47 achieved dominance and out-performed the Fw 190 by 500 ft/min. Dives of 65 degrees were carried out from 10,000 ft to 3,000 ft, starting at 250 mph IAS. Once again the Fw 190 held an initial advantage but was passed by the P-47 at 3,000 ft at a much greater speed.

At speeds in excess of 250 mph IAS, the two aircraft were turned on each other's tail as tight as possible and alternating the turns left and right. The P-47 easily out-turned the Fw 190 at 10,000 ft and had to throttle back to keep from overshooting, a level of superiority that increased with altitude. It was found that the Fw 190 was very heavy in terms of fore and aft control, vibrated excessively, and tended to black out its pilot. Below 250 mph IAS however, the ability of the Fw 190 to hang on its propeller and turn inside the P-47 was very evident. The Fw 190 was also able to accelerate suddenly and change to a more favourable position.

Close-up of the left side of MP499's BMW 801D-2 showing exhaust grouping and cooling slots.

Another view of MP499, this time with background detail intact. It appears that the secret aircraft the censor had been trying to hide in earlier photos was an old Vickers Wellesley!

The concluding remarks of the USAAF report were as follows :

## USAAF opinion

'The 190 performs nicely in all aerobatic manoeuvres with the exception of a very slight fore and aft control which makes low altitude manoeuvres dangerous. This aircraft has an extremely bad high speed stall in turns which is not so evident in high speed pull outs, but if trimmed and pulled hard enough it will spin violently straight down without warning. Aileron control is very good at all speeds and rudder control is normally good. Forward and side visibility are very good while rear visibility is very poor. The cockpit is uncomfortably small for a pilot taller than 5 ft 11 in. Baling out would be difficult for any pilot. The aircraft is quite nose heavy which would make dead stick landings dangerous and high speed dives near the ground dangerous. The engine seems to run rough at all times and the vibration transmitted through the control column almost completely destroys any feel of the flying characteristics. This characteristic is partly responsible for the lack of warning in high speed stalls.'

To show how the Fw 190 was used by the *Luftwaffe* to obtain the maximum advantage in fighter v fighter combat it is necessary to return to the summer of 1942. Although the Fw 190 was rather suspect at altitude and could not hope to stay with a Spitfire in a sustained turn, its good points far out-weighed the bad and as long as the aircraft was operated to its strengths, it had little to fear. In addition to its excellent climb performance, the Fw 190 allowed the various elements of JG 2 and 26 to be based away from the French coast which allowed them to gain height and manoeuvre into an attacking position free from the attentions of the RAF. With a superior aircraft and height to spare, the timing of an attack (if it came at all) was entirely in the hands of the *Experten* leading the German formations. On many occasions they were content to keep a watching brief. Only when a particular operation demanded a response or when some elements of the RAF's Wing formations became detached could an attack be virtually

Detail of the starboard undercarriage leg of MP499. The Fw 190 was unusual in having an electrically activated undercarriage (and flaps). This imposed a considerable load on the aircraft's battery and although the normal procedure was to lower flaps first and then the undercarriage, some RAF pilots testing captured Fw 190s preferred to get the gear down first in case flap activation flattened the battery.

guaranteed. Occasionally they did launch an attack on an entire Wing, one of the most devastating taking place on 1 June 1942 which highlights the Fw 190's main advantages and the way it was used to best effect.

The day dawned bright and sunny, ideal weather for the RAF's 'Circus' operations which were intended to draw the German fighters into a battle of attrition. Following a morning sweep by two Wings of Spitfires which were left to go on their way, further

activity was noted in the early afternoon. This was Circus 178 which took eight Hurricane fighter-bombers to Bruges in Belgium with an escort of fourteen squadrons of Spitfires. Acting as target support was the Debden Wing, comprising 65, 71, 111 and 350 Squadrons.

Led by Wing Commander J.A.G. Gordon, the Wing's forty-six Spitfire Vs had taken off from Debden and the satellite airfield at Great Sampford between 1245–1255 hrs before forming up and crossing the English coast at Deal at 1312 hrs. As the Wing began its climb over the Channel to make a landfall at Thourout, its progress was monitored on German radar screens and the *Geschwader Stab* and the First and Third *Gruppe* of JG 26 were ordered to scramble at 1320 hrs and climb as quickly as possible in the direction of Ostend. No attempt was made to intercept the larger RAF formation which included the Hurricane bombers, instead the defending Fw 190s were vectored towards the Debden Wing which by now had 65 Squadron in the low position at 20,000 ft with 111, 71 and 350 Squadrons stepped up above and behind at 22,000, 23,000 and 25,000 ft respectively.

As the Spitfires curved towards Bruges, condensation trails could be seen a few thousand feet above and to the south as the Fw 190s watched and waited. The attack did not materialise until the Wing was on its way out near Blankenburge, but when it came, it was timed to perfection and delivered with devastating effect.

## Diving attack

It was carried out under the watchful eye of *Major* Gerhard Schopfel who dispatched a small number of Fw 190s to dive through the RAF formation, a tactic that succeeded in breaking up the Wing's cohesion as the Spitfires broke into the supposed attack. Before they could re-form, *Hauptmann* Johannes Seifert at the head of I *Gruppe* saw his opportunity. Launching a diving attack he first went for the out-of-position 111 Squadron and soon the Spitfires flown by Sergeants R.C. Bryson and W.H. Cumming were shot down. Continuing his dive Seifert then went for the low squadron (Number 65) and his pilots quickly sent Wing Commander Gordon and his wingman

RAF personnel mix with 'men from the ministry' as they discover the Fw 190's secrets. The triangular door in the left side of the fin allowed access to the rudder cables and tailwheel retraction system.

Sergeant R.E. Parrack spinning to the ground. Having seized the initiative the attack was continued over the Channel where *Oberleutnant* Johannes Schmidt shot down Pilot Officer J.R. Richards into the sea (to be rescued by a British motor launch) and severely damaged the aircraft flown by Sergeant V. Kopacek.

## Top cover bounced

As Seifert's men were wreaking havoc with the low squadrons, *Hauptmann* Josef 'Pips' Priller's III *Gruppe* began its own diving attack on the top cover Spitfires. Within the first few seconds 350 Squadron had Flight Sergeant G.J.Livyns and Sergeant J.L. Hansez shot down, whilst 71 Squadron lost Pilot Officer E.G. Teicheira. By now the Debden Wing had lost its cohesion completely and individual combats continued down to ground level, the final RAF loss being Pilot Officer Bobby Laumans of 350 Squadron who was outnumbered five to one:

'Between each engagement I tried to fly a few miles towards England as it was obvious that I couldn't shoot down all of the Germans. It was also obvious that they wouldn't let me go! My petrol was going down fast but it was no good trying to flee as the Fw 190 was faster than the Spitfire V so I faced them each time they attacked. Finally, when I was firing at one of the enemy in front of me, two of his comrades attacked from astern, one left, one right. A shell suddenly entered my cockpit from the left-hand side, pierced the dashboard and exploded in the petrol tank in front. My aircraft was immediately set on fire and the only thing I could do was to bale out. The combat had started at around 25,000 ft and I abandoned the aircraft at 900 ft, ending up in the sea somewhere between Ostend and Dover.'

After spending 63 hours in his dinghy,

This view of MP499 shows the early tail fixing for the radio antenna and ground adjustable rudder tab. The tab was marked *Nicht Verstellen* (do not adjust). The tailplane could be adjusted in flight through 5 degrees via an electric motor for trim control in pitch.

Laumans was picked up by the Germans and was eventually sent to *Stalag Luft* III at Sagen.

RAF losses amounted to nine aircraft destroyed (approximately 20 per cent of the total Wing strength), five pilots killed, one missing, two PoWs and one wounded. Despite claims of three Fw 190s destroyed, no JG 26 aircraft had even been damaged.

This particular operation illustrated the Fw 190 at its best. Even though JG 26 had been scrambled half an hour after the RAF fighters had taken off, there was still ample time to

Another view of the cockpit of Faber's Fw 190A-3. Of note is the well laid out side console containing electrical circuit breakers. A particularly neat touch is the slot that forms a map holder between the vertical face of the console and the control column. The silver knob above the console is the canopy crank handle.

Captured Fw 190A-4/U8 PE882 is escorted by Spitfire Va L1096 (Y2-W) and Spitfire I R7193 (Y1-M) from RNAS Yeovilton. Such escorts were often necessary, to prevent attacks by other Allied fighters.

climb to a height of around 28,000 ft and for the German formations to be vectored to a suitable position up-sun to survey the scene below them. Although the Debden Wing had maintained its shape, Schopfel knew that a feint diving attack could be carried out with very little risk and that it might open up

opportunities for the majority of his force which he held in reserve. This proved to be the case when 111 Squadron lost its position within the Wing allowing Seifert to attack both it and 65 Squadron. With their attention distracted by what was going on below them, the high cover squadrons could then be attacked by Priller's

Fw 190A-4/U8 *Werke* Nr 5843, formerly of SKG 10, under new management as PN999. This aircraft was tested by the Royal Aircraft Establishment before being delivered to 1426 (Enemy Aircraft) Flight. It was last recorded as being in store at 47 MU Sealand in November 1947.

A rarely seen sight that one day might be repeated at an airshow. Fw 190A-4 PM679 carries out a low level beat up with P-47D Thunderbolt W-QP of the 334th Fighter Squadron, 4th Fighter Group, Eighth Air Force.

III *Gruppe*, which again used the Fw 190's chief asset, its speed in the dive.

It was also no coincidence that the attack had been carried out towards the end of the Debden Wing's sweep, as the German pilots knew that their counterparts would be casting anxious glances at their petrol gauges and that combat at this stage would seriously erode precious fuel reserves.

In such a situation a Spitfire pilot was likely to play into his opposite number's hands by attempting to dive for home, as any attempt to

mix it would most likely result in there being insufficient fuel to make it back to base.

The entire attack from start to finish lasted around ten minutes with the majority of the Spitfires shot down being dispatched within the first few seconds of each engagement.

Successful German pilots included *Major* Schopfel, who was credited with his 40th victory, *Hauptmann* Seifert (35th), *Hauptmann* Priller (73rd), and *Leutnant* Paul Galland, brother of the more famous Adolf, who shot down his eleventh victim.

Another ex-SKG 10 machine, PE882 was an Fw 190A-4/U8 *Werke* Nr 7155 that landed in error at West Malling on the night of 17 April 1943. Transferred to 1426 (Enemy Aircraft) Flight, it was lost in a crash on 13 October 1944, which took the life of the Flight's commander, Flight Lieutenant E.R. Lewendon.

# 5. Multi-role Fighter: Versions and Variants

The Fw 190 was produced in numerous variants, each tailored to a particular role and operational environment. In addition there were many sub-variants which were divided into two categories, the letter 'U' (for *Umbau* or rebuilding) signifying a conversion carried out by the manufacturer. 'R' (for *Rustsatz*) indicated a set of parts that were used to modify aircraft in the field.

This chapter details the principal model variations and the widely differing weapons configurations that were used.

### Fw 190A-1

The Fw 190A-1 was similar to the long-spanned V-5g and was powered by a 1,600 hp BMW 801C-1 with four 7.92 mm MG 17 machine guns (two mounted above the engine and two in the wing roots) plus two 20 mm MG FF cannon in the outer wings and an FuG 7a radio. Differences between the A-1 and the earlier A-0 model included under-wing blisters to accommodate the ammunition drums of the MG FF cannon, a revised blister of flattened top section on the left-hand engine cowling for the supercharger ducting, two reinforcing struts to the pilot's headrest and a slightly elongated spinner. Some later Fw 190A-1s featured the BMW 801D radial of 1,700 hp in which case vertical slots were cut into the fuselage sides just aft of the exhaust gas efflux to aid cooling.

### Fw 190A-2

Apart from chronic engine unreliability, the main problem with the A-1 was its lack of hitting power, a weakness that was remedied in the A-2 by the provision of two 20 mm MG 151/20 cannon in place of the MG 17s in the wing roots. To accommodate the new guns a raised blister was required on the upper wing root for the larger gun breeches. The MG 17s mounted over the engine were retained as were the outer MG FF cannon, although some pilots preferred to have these removed to improve performance. Power was provided by either the BMW 801C or D, cooling slots again being used on those aircraft fitted with the latter. Other features included a small ventrally mounted aerial for the FuG 25 IFF (Identification Friend or Foe) radio, and a single headrest strut, although a number of A-2s still retained the twin strut arrangement as used on the A-1.

### Fw 190A-3

Virtually the same as the A-2, the A-3 was powered by the BMW 801D-1 or D-2 and was the first to receive the ventral ETC 501 rack in the A-3/U1 and A-3/U3 sub-variants. These were used to carry a 300-litre (66-gallon) drop tank or an SC 250/SC 500 bomb (the number indicating the bomb's weight in kilogrammes). The A-3/U4 reconnaissance machine had the outboard cannon removed and two Rb 12 cameras mounted in the rear fuselage and the A-3/U7 high altitude fighter had twin nose-mounted air intakes to increase air flow to the supercharger.

### Fw 190A-4

The A-4 was similar to the A-3 except that it had an upgraded radio installation with a FuG 16 set replacing the old FuG 7. This resulted in an identifying feature in the shape of a small triangular post mounted on top of the fin for

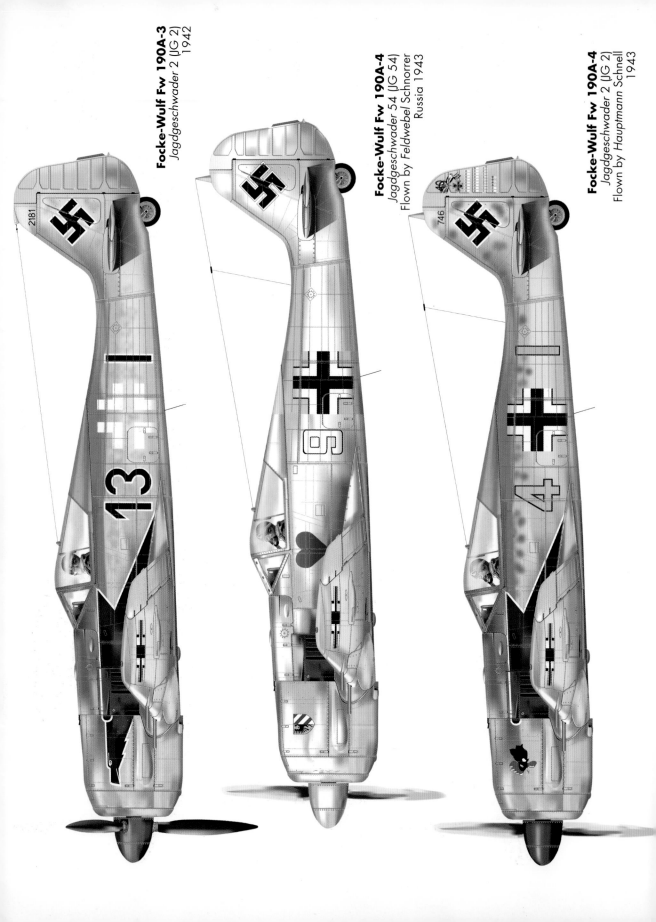

**Focke-Wulf Fw 190A-3**
*Jagdgeschwader 2 (JG 2)*
1942

**Focke-Wulf Fw 190A-4**
*Jagdgeschwader 54 (JG 54)*
*Flown by Feldwebel Schnorrer*
*Russia 1943*

**Focke-Wulf Fw 190A-4**
*Jagdgeschwader 2 (JG 2)*
*Flown by Hauptmann Schnell*
1943

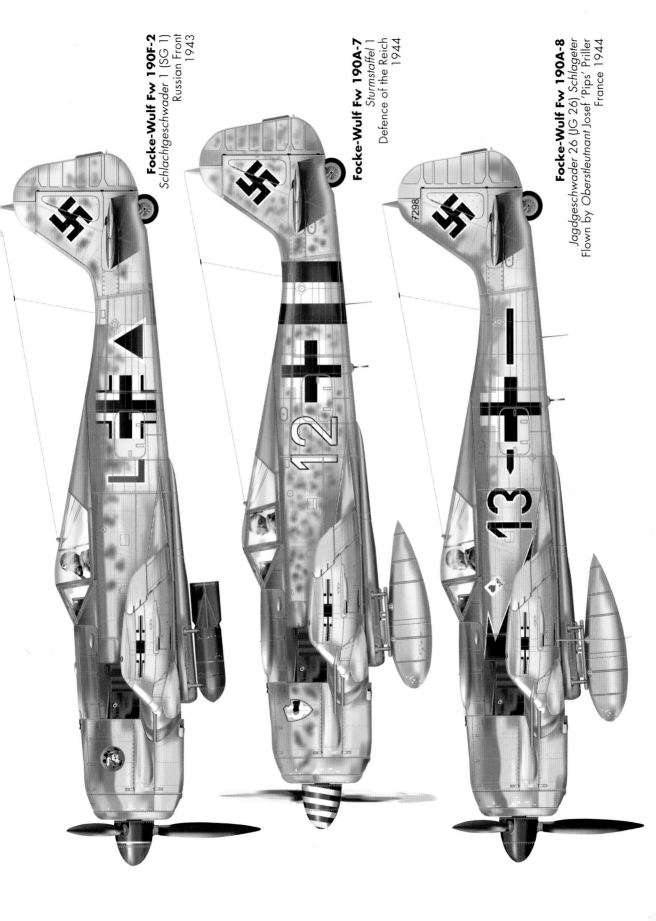

**Focke-Wulf Fw 190F-2**
*Schlachtgeschwader 1 (SG 1)*
Russian Front
1943

**Focke-Wulf Fw 190A-7**
*Sturmstaffel 1*
Defence of the Reich
1944

**Focke-Wulf Fw 190A-8**
*Jagdgeschwader 26 (JG 26) Schlageter*
Flown by Oberstleutnant Josef 'Pips' Priller
France 1944

An early pre-production Fw 190V-5k *Werke* Nr 0006. Of the first A-0 aircraft *Werke* Nrs 0006–0014 were designated as V-5k with the smaller wing, whereas *Werke* Nrs 0015–0035 were classified as V-5g and were fitted with wings of slightly increased span and greater area. This aircraft is factory fresh apart from the exhaust staining which is already beginning to appear on the fuselage side.

the radio antenna. Power still came from the BMW 801D-1 or D-2, the familiar cooling slots giving way to pilot-operated gills on later examples, and late production A-4s were the first Fw 190s to have MW-50 injection which boosted power to 2,100 hp for short periods, allowing a speed of 416 mph to be reached at 20,600 ft. The habit of removing the small centrally mounted undercarriage doors on bomb-carrying versions (first seen on the A-3) became more widespread with the A-4. Another minor modification was the introduction of wider headrest armour, although this could also be seen on some late A-3s. Main sub-variants were the A-4/U1, a night-capable fighter-bomber with ETC 501 rack, port wing-mounted landing light and exhaust flame 'blinkers'; the A-4/U3, a ground attack machine with outer cannon removed and an ETC 501 rack for an SC 250/SC 500 bomb; the reconnaissance A-4/U4, similar to the A-3/U4; and the A-4/U-8, a long-range fighter-bomber armed only with inboard MG 151s but possessing a ventral ETC 501 rack and the ability to carry 300-litre fuel tanks under each wing. Principal *Rustsatz* sub-variants were the A-4/R1 with FuG 16ZE radio and the A-4/R6 with underwing WGr 21 rocket launchers.

## Fw 190A-5

Although again similar to its immediate predecessor, the A-5 had a revised engine mounting which allowed the BMW 801D-2 to be moved forward by 6 in to help alleviate engine overheating. The armament still comprised twin engine-mounted MG 17s, wing root-mounted MG 151 cannon with outboard MG FFs, although once again the latter were frequently deleted to improve performance. There were many sub-variants of the A-5, some of which remained as projects, while others acted as development aircraft for future variants. Of those that were produced, the A-5/U2 was a night fighter-bomber with the usual night equipment of exhaust 'blinkers' and landing light, plus ventral ETC 501 rack and 300-litre tanks under each wing, while the

FOCKE-WULF FW 190A

A publicity photo of an Fw 190A on a test flight. The semi retractable tailwheel is evident, as is the large amount of cockpit glazing behind the pilot's seat that gave the Fw 190 better all-round vision than virtually every other contemporary fighter. This visibility was commented on favourably by Allied pilots who flew captured examples.

A-5/U-3 was a ground support fighter which could carry a wide variety of bombs including a centrally mounted SC 250/SC 500 and four wing-mounted SC 50 bombs or a total of eight SC 50s. The U8 was another *Jabo-Rei* (fighter-bomber) with the same offensive equipment as the A-4/U8. The A-5/R1 and A-5/R6 had FuG 16ZE radio and WGr 21 rocket launchers respectively, as on the A-4.

**Fw 190A-6**

By now the all-up weight of the Fw 190 had begun to rise alarmingly, due mainly to increased weaponry and additional armour (in the case of the A-5/U3 this amounted to 893 lb). This was addressed with the A-6, which featured a revised wing of increased strength as tested on the A-5/U10. The other notable feature of the A-6 was the replacement of the MG FF cannon in the outer wings with a further pair of MG 151/20s. Sub-variants included the A-6/R1, which had the outboard guns replaced by two under-wing WB 151 containers, each with a pair of MG 151/20

cannon, and the A-6/R2 which used the 30-mm MK 108 cannon in the wing container instead of the twin MG 151 installation. The A-6/R3 featured a 30-mm MK-103 cannon in each under-wing gondola and the A-6/R6 saw the under-wing cannon armament replaced by WGr 21 rocket launchers. Following night operations with the A-5/U2 as *Wilde Sau* fighters against the RAF's heavy bombers, some A-6s were modified to carry FuG 216 *Neptun* radar equipment and its associated whip aerial arrays, exhaust 'blinkers' and flash suppressors for the fuselage-mounted guns.

**Fw 190A-7**

Only eighty examples of the Fw 190A-7 were produced, its most notable feature being the replacement of the engine-mounted MG 17 machine-guns with 13-mm MG 131s. To accommodate the new installation, the upper access panel had to be revised as the MG 131 was a much bulkier weapon, the resulting front fuselage profile showing a pronounced bulge on the top surface and half-way down the side.

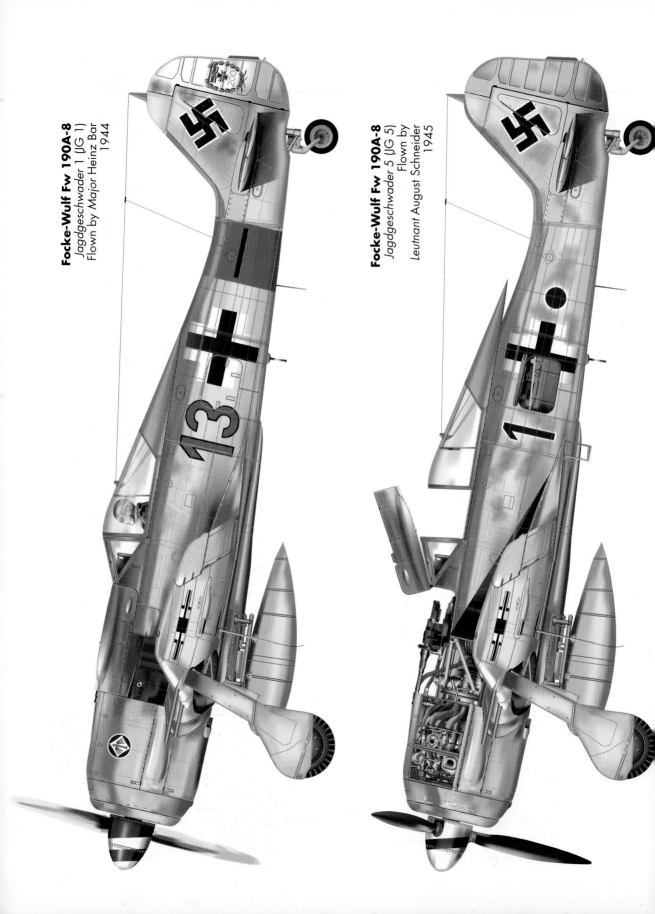

**Focke-Wulf Fw 190A-8**
*Jagdgeschwader 1 (JG 1)*
Flown by Major Heinz Bar
1944

**Focke-Wulf Fw 190A-8**
*Jagdgeschwader 5 (JG 5)*
Flown by
Leutnant August Schneider
1945

**Focke-Wulf Fw 190F-8**
*Schlachtgeschwader 4 (SG 4)*
*Italy*
*1944*

**Focke-Wulf Fw 190A-8**
*Jagdgeschwader 3 (JG 3)*
*Flown by*
*Major Walter Dahl*
*1944*

The guns also had to be mounted further apart and as a result the mounting structure was redesigned and strengthened to accommodate them. Due to the wider spacing of the blast troughs, the toggle fasteners for the cowling had to be moved to the side panels. The A-7 also introduced the more advanced Revi 16B gunsight in place of the Revi 12C/D. Like the A-6, wing armament comprised four MG 151/20 cannon. The *Rustsatz* kits produced for the A-7 resulted in the R1, R2, R3 and R6 and were the same as used on the A-6.

## Fw 190A-8

In contrast to the A-7, the A-8 was built in large numbers and had the benefit of either MW-50 water-methanol or GM-1 nitrous-oxide boost, the tanks for these being located behind the pilot's seat. If required these could be deleted

and replaced by an additional fuel tank of 25 gallons capacity. The A-8 was the only variant to be modified as a two-seater, the A-8/U1 being intended as a precursor of the Fw 190S, but in the event this was not proceeded with and only three A-8s were converted as trainers. The A-8/U3 was designated as the upper half of the *Mistel* combination and the A-8/U11 was a fighter-bomber which in addition to the usual combinations of bombs could also carry the BT 700 torpedo bomb. Like the A-6, the A-8 was used as a night-fighter with either FuG 216 or FuG 217 *Neptun* radar systems. The sub-variants R1–R6 were similar to those of the A-6, but several other *Rustsatz* sets were produced, including the R7 which had a specially armoured cockpit for use by the *Sturmstaffel*. This consisted of increased protection for the

Although most of the engine was accessible via hinged panels, construction tolerances were of a very high order so that ease of maintenance did not come at the expense of aerodynamic drag. The exceptionally smooth contours of the engine cowling is evident in this photo of an early production Fw 190A-1, probably *Werke* Nr 067. The A-1 also featured a slightly longer spinner than the A-0.

The Focke-Wulf flight line preparing to start another busy day. The Fw 190 in the foreground is *Werke* Nr 0015, one of the pre-production V-5 series and the first aircraft to receive the larger wing.

MG 131 machine-guns, the fuselage sides and thicker armoured glass to the canopy and windscreen. The R8 was armed with two MK 108 cannon, as on the R2, together with the extra armour plate of the R7. The R11 and R12 were to have been all-weather fighters with PKS-12 radio navigation equipment but never got beyond the project stage.

### Fw 190A-9

The A-9 variant was powered by a BMW 801F engine of 2,000 hp but only one machine, V-34 *Werke* Nr 410230, was produced. Intended as a ramming fighter, it featured armoured wing leading edges and production examples would have carried a single 30 mm MK 108 cannon in each of the outer wings and been powered by a BMW 801TS engine with turbo-supercharging. The proposed R11 and R12 sub-variants were all-weather fighters equipped with PKS-12.

### Fw 190A-10

Last in the A-series, the A-10 was a projected model which did not get past the drawing board. Intended as another fighter-bomber variant, it was to have been powered by a BMW 801TS/TH engine and armament would have consisted of two engine-mounted MG 131s, two MG 151/20s in the wing roots with either two MG 151/20s or two MK 108s in the outer wing positions. A ventral ETC 503 rack and the under-wing hardpoints would have allowed a total bomb load of 3,860 lb or the carriage of three 300-litre overload tanks.

### Fw 190B-0/B-1

The proposed B-series was Focke-Wulf's first attempt to turn the Fw 190 into a true high-performance high altitude fighter. The first B-0 machine was a re-worked A-1 (*Werke* Nr 0046) which featured a revised wing of 40 ft 4 in span and 218.5 sq ft area but no armament. It also had a pressurised cabin with double glazing and GM-1 boost. Three further development aircraft appeared (*Werke* Nrs 0047, 0048 and 0055) but these possessed standard wings. Only one B-1 was produced (a conversion of A-1 *Werke* Nr 811). Although originally intended to have armament of 4 x MG 17 and 2 x MG FF, the sole B-1 was fitted with 2 x MG 17, 2 x MG 151 and 2 x MG FF. Continual difficulties during testing in the first half of 1943 led to the B-series being abandoned.

### Fw 190C-0/C-1

Following the demise of the Fw 190B, priority shifted to the C-series which had similar design aims and was ultimately to suffer the same fate. The first prototype (V-13 *Werke* Nr 0036) was powered by a Daimler-Benz DB 603A engine of 1,750 hp but, other than its annular radiator, was similar structurally to A-series machines. The next in line (V-18 *Werke* Nr 0040) was radically different and featured a DB 603G with Hirth turbo-supercharger, four-blade VDM propeller and a pressurised cabin. Although the wing remained as standard, the fuselage length was increased to 31 ft 1 in and there was a large

**Focke-Wulf Fw 190F-8**
*Schlachtgeschwader 2 (SG 2)*
1945

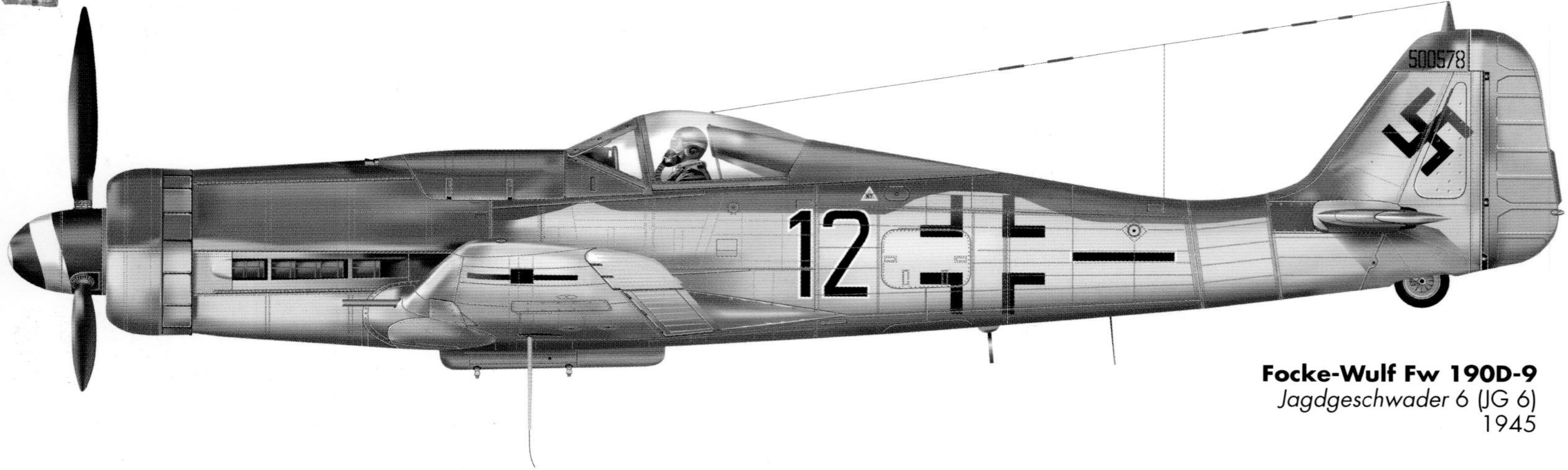

**Focke-Wulf Fw 190D-9**
*Jagdgeschwader 6 (JG 6)*
1945

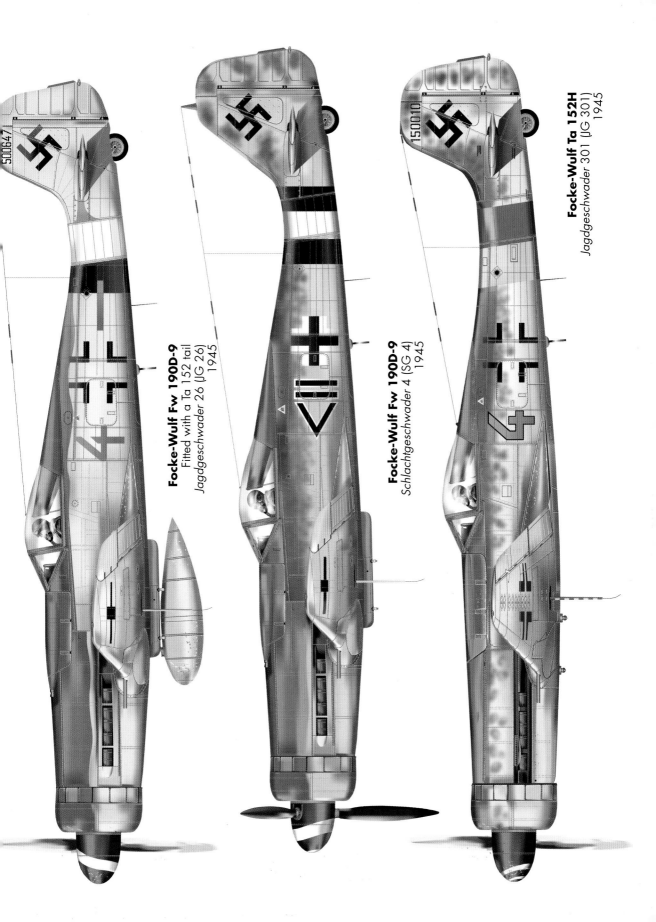

**Focke-Wulf Fw 190D-9**
Fitted with a Ta 152 tail
Jagdgeschwader 26 (JG 26)
1945

**Focke-Wulf Fw 190D-9**
Schlachtgeschwader 4 (SG 4)
1945

**Focke-Wulf Ta 152H**
Jagdgeschwader 301 (JG 301)
1945

Fw 190V-18 *Werke* Nr 0040 CF+OY. This view of the second prototype of the Fw 190C shows the large ventral intake for the Hirth turbo-blower to advantage, and the enlarged tail surfaces that were manufactured in wood. Although the turbo-blower worked satisfactorily, Germany's shortage of high quality metals led to severe difficulties with regard to reliability, as the ducting was unable to withstand high exhaust gas temperatures. Development led to only a modest improvement and the system was eventually abandoned.

ventral intake for the blower which led to the nickname 'Kangaroo'. Because of the increased blade area the vertical tail surfaces were of broader chord. Five further prototypes followed, the last in line being equipped with two MG 131 machine-guns and two MG 151/20 cannon, but severe problems with the turbo-supercharger ducting led to the C-series also being cancelled.

### Fw 190D-9

First of the long-nose Fw 190s, the D-9 was designated as such as it followed on from the A-8 on the production lines. It featured the same wing as used on the A-8, but its 1,750 hp Junkers Jumo 213A liquid-cooled engine was mated to an extended fuselage of 33 ft 5 in. Early production machines were fitted with the standard canopy but later examples had the bulged hood that was a feature of late F-series aircraft. Apart from early aircraft, most were fitted with MW-50 boost which increased power to 2,240 hp. The armament comprised two MG 131 machine-guns mounted over the engine and two MG 151/20 cannon in the wing roots. Provision was also made for a ventral ETC 504 rack for the carriage of bombs or overload tanks. The D-9/R11 was an all-weather fighter with the same armament plus PKS 12 radio navigation equipment, FuG 125 and heated windows, although lack of availability of the D/F equipment meant that very few R11 sub-variants were built.

### Fw 190D-10

The D-10 variant was not put into production and only two re-worked D-9s (*Werke* Nrs 210001 and 210002) were designated as such. The major difference between the D-10 and its predecessor was the deletion of the engine-mounted MG 131 guns which were replaced by a single 30-mm MK 108 cannon firing through the spinner.

### Fw 190D-11

Powered by the Jumo 213F engine with MW-50 injection, the D-11 did not get beyond the testing of seven prototypes, four of which were rebuilt A-8s. The D-11 dispensed with the

Fw 190V-53 *Werke* Nr 170003 was the second prototype for the D-9 and followed the V-17/U1. It was powered by a Jumo 213A in-line engine, and had standard armament of two engine-mounted MG 131 heavy machine-guns and two wing root MG 151/20 cannon, plus two additional MG 151/20s in the outer wings. Prominent in this view are the wide-chord propeller blades.

engine-mounted guns in favour of two MG 151/20 cannon in the wing roots with two MK 108s in the outer wing positions. Had the aircraft gone into production it is likely that two sub-variants would have emerged, the D-11/R20 with PKS-12 directional control and the D-11/R21 with PKS 12 and FuG 125 *Hermine* D/F.

### Fw 190D-12

Intended as a ground-attack fighter, the D-12 was to have been produced in four different versions although only a small number had been completed by the end of the war. First in the series was the D-12/R5 with Jumo 213F and MW-50, although this engine was to have been replaced by the Jumo 213EB. The armament consisted of a single engine-mounted MK 108 cannon and two MK 151/20s in the wing roots. Fuel capacity was boosted by four extra fuel tanks in the wings which together contained 69 gallons. Next in line was the D-12/R11 which was designated as an all-weather fighter and was equipped with PKS-12 and FuG 125. A few were produced by Arado and Fieseler in March

1945. The last two Fw 190D-12s were projects only. The D-12/R21 was similar to the D-12/R11 but without PKS-12 and FuG 125. The D-12/R25 was similar to the D-12/R5 and would have been powered by the Jumo 213EB.

### Fw 190D-13

The only major difference between the D-13 and the D-12 was the deletion of the engine-mounted MK 108 cannon, which was replaced by an MG 151/20. Only two prototypes were built, both being rebuilt A-8s (V-62 *Werke* Nr 732053 and V-71 *Werke* Nr 732054). The D-13 was powered by the Jumo 213F although like the D-12, this engine would have been replaced by the Jumo 213EB. Had this version gone into production it is likely that D-13 sub-variants would have been the same as for the D-12.

### Fw 190D-14

The D-14 appeared only as two prototypes, V-76, a converted D-9 (*Werke* Nr 210040), and V-77 which was a rebuild of D-12 *Werke* Nr 200043. Although generally similar to other aircraft in this series, the D-14 had a Daimler-Benz DB 603E engine which required minor

Fw 190F-8/R14, seen here as Air Ministry 111 at Farnborough in 1945, was developed as a torpedo-carrier and was powered by a BMW 801TU. One of its most noticeable features is a raised tailwheel to allow adequate ground clearance for the fins of the torpedo which extended to a point midway between cockpit and tailplane. The torpedo was carried on an ETC 502 rack with armament limited to two engine-mounted MG 131 machine-guns. Production did not get under way before the end of the war.

modification work to be carried out in relation to the engine-mounted gun and alterations to oil tanks, the MW-50 injection installation and engine instruments. If the D-14 had gone into production it would most probably have used a DB 603LA. Armament was to have been as used on the D-12 – one MK 108 cannon with two MG 151/20s located in the wing roots.

### Fw 190D-15

Last in the D-series, the D-15 was again to have been powered by a DB 603LA and built using A-8/F-8 airframes. An all-weather version, the D-15/R11, would have been equipped with PKS-12, FuG 125 and heated windows but the end of hostilities in Europe meant that it never got beyond the project stage.

### Fw 190E-1

This variant was to have been a reconnaissance fighter based around the conversion of Fw 190A-4 airframes and utilising a pair of Rb 12 cameras, but as the requirement was being met successfully by the U4 sub-variants of the A-3 and A-5, its development was stillborn and it did not progress beyond the project stage.

### Fw 190F-1

As experience was gained with the A-series in the *Jabo* role, it was quickly realised that the Fw 190 was well suited to replace the *Luftwaffe*'s ageing Ju 87 Stukas. As a dedicated ground-attack machine the Fw 190F was equipped with additional armour to protect the underside of the fuselage including the BMW 801D-2 engine and the centre-section fuel tanks. Many later F-series aircraft featured a bulged cockpit hood which was adopted to allow sufficient space for the pilot's revised headrest armour. Standard armament was reduced to two engine-mounted MG 17 machine-guns and two MG 151/20 cannon in the wing roots. The F-1, the first in the series, was produced in small numbers and could be operated with an ETC 501 bomb rack under the fuselage and two ETC 50 racks under

Fw 190G-3 DN+FP was captured by US forces at the end of the war and was returned to the USA for trials. The Fw 190F and G were ground-attack versions of the Fw 190A, the G-series appearing in service before the more extensively modified F. The G-1 was based on the A-4/U8 with the G-2 and G-3 being developed from the A-5/A-6 with its revised engine mounting and extended nose. The G-8 was similar to the A-8 and F-8.

each wing. As the F-1 was a re-worked A-4/U3, it had the original 'short' A-series fuselage, whereas the F-2 and subsequent aircraft had the longer fuselage of the A-5.

### Fw 190F-2

The F-2 had the same offensive capability of the F-1 except that many were to feature the ER 4 multiple bomb rack which could be used to carry four SC 50 bombs under the fuselage. As most F-2s were used on the Eastern Front many were to be seen fitted with nose-mounted air intakes incorporating sand filters.

### Fw 190F-3

Several sub-variants of the F-3 (the U3 and U14 torpedo-fighters and the U4 and U5 ground-attack fighters) did not proceed beyond the project stage and most F-3s were either R1 or R3 *Rustsatz* conversions. The F-3/R1 featured ETC 50 under-wing racks fitted with special streamlined fairings and the F-3/R-3 was capable of carrying a 30-mm MK 103 cannon under each wing.

### Fw 190F-8

As the F-4, F-5, F-6 and F-7 ground-attack variants did not go into production, it was the F-8 that appeared next. Based on the A-8 it differed from previous aircraft in the F-series in having MG 131 machine-guns mounted over the engine and it also featured a number of modifications including a revised release system which gave the pilot the opportunity to select the number of bombs to be used and allowed the opportunity of attacking multiple targets. Several *Umbau* versions of the F-8 were not proceeded with including the F-8/U1 trainer, the F-8/U2 and F-8/U3 which were to have been armed with one BT 1400 torpedo, and the F-8/U14 which was to have carried an LTF 5a torpedo. Although many *Rustsatz* conversions were planned, only the F-8/R1 was produced in any great number, this particular sub-variant featuring ETC 50 racks under each wing, later replaced by ETC 71s. Only two F-8/R3s were built. The standard armament was augmented by two underwing MK 103 cannon and had the war continued this version would have been used for long-range attack using a 300-litre fuel tank carried in the ventral position with ETC 503 racks under the wings. Of the other sub-variants, the MK 108-armed F-8/R2 was not built and the F-8/R5, which carried 25 gallons extra fuel in the rear fuselage, was cancelled in late 1944. The night-attack F-8/R13 powered by a BMW 801TS and the similarly engined F-8/R14, F-8/R15 and F-8/R16 torpedo aircraft could not be put into production before the end of the war.

**Fw 190F-9**

The F-9 was produced in small numbers towards the end of the war and differed from the F-8 principally in having a 2,200 hp BMW 801TS engine. Its operational capability could be varied by use of the same *Rustsatz* conversions as produced for the F-8.

**Fw 190F-10/16**

Intended as ground support fighters, only the F-15 prototype (V-66 *Werke* Nr 584002) was completed. This had the A-8 wing, a BMW 801TS/TH engine and a revised undercarriage incorporating larger wheels. It was armed with two MG 131s over the engine, two MG 151/20s in the wing roots and an ETC 504 rack.

**Fw 190G-1**

G-series aircraft followed on from the early *Jabo-Rei* conversions of the A-series, the G-1 being based on the A-4/U8. It normally carried two 300-litre tanks on 'streamlined' fairings under the wings with an ETC 501 bomb rack under the fuselage. As speed and long range were the prime requirements, the armament was reduced to a pair of MG 151/20s in the wing roots, the blast troughs for the engine-mounted guns being faired over.

**Fw 190G-2**

As the G-2 was based on the A-5/U8, it had the longer fuselage of that variant. The offensive load was similar to the G-1 except that the G-2 normally had its overload tanks mounted on unfaired Messerschmitt supports which actually produced less drag than the faired Junkers type used on the G-1. Some G-2s featured modified flame dampers for night operations, and were referred to as G-2/N.

**Fw 190G-3**

The G-3 was externally similar to its predecessors but featured yet another variation in under-wing racks. These fairings were produced by Focke-Wulf and extended from the leading edge approximately to half-chord with longitudinal outriggers. As bombs could be carried on these racks, the G-3 could be used in a variety of roles and if necessary could be used to attack short-range targets with a centrally mounted SC 500 and two SC 250s under the wings. Like the G-2, a few aircraft were modified for operations at night becoming G-3/Ns, and a small number of aircraft were designated G-3/R1 and were equipped with ETC 50 bomb racks under the wings.

**Fw 190G-8**

The G-8 was closely related to the A-8 and F-8 but continued the G-series trend by only having two MG 151/20s in the wing roots. There was little to distinguish the G-8 from the G-3 except that the pitot tube was moved from a mid-wing position to the wingtip and ETC 503 bomb racks were generally fitted under the wings. Internally an additional 25-gallon fuel tank or a tank for GM-1 nitrous-oxide injection was installed. Towards the end of the war a number were converted as G-8/R5s by fitting ETC 71 under-wing racks for SC 50 bombs.

**Ta 152A-1/A-2**

Generally similar to the Fw 190D-9, neither variant got past the project stage. Power would have come from a Jumo 213A and armament would have comprised four MG 151/20 cannon. It was also intended to fit FuG 24 radio in place of FuG 16.

**Ta 152B-1/B-5**

The B-1 and B-2 fighters, the B-3 ground support fighter and the B-4 heavy fighter remained as projects so that the only B-series aircraft to be produced before the end of the war was the first B-5 (V-68 *Werke* Nr 170003) which was a rebuild of V-53 (a former D-9

Fw 190V-32 *Werke* Nr 0057 registered GH+KV was built as an A-0 and took part in the programme to develop the Fw 190C before being modified again as the V-32/U1 for the proposed Ta 153 high-altitude fighter. The Ta 153 was abandoned in favour of the Ta 152 as the need to produce new construction jigs would have caused unacceptable production delays.

prototype) and three all-weather B-5/R11s (V-19, V-20 and V-21) which were armed with three MK 103 cannon.

**Ta 152C-0/C-4**

The Ta 152C did see service, although only in very small numbers. The C-0 and C-1 were both powered by the 2,100 hp Daimler-Benz DB 603L and were armed with one MK 108 and four MG 151/20s. The C-2 was identical, apart from having a DB 603LA and a revised radio fit, while the C-3 was fitted with an engine-mounted MK 103 cannon in place of the MK 108. The final Ta 152 in the C-series was the C-4 which was not produced but would have featured under-wing WGr 21 rocket launchers.

**Ta 152E-0/E-2**

The Ta 152E was meant to be a reconnaissance machine, with a Jumo 213E engine and either an Rb 75/30 camera (E-1) or an Rb 50/18 (E-1/R1). The E-2 would have featured the extended wing of the Ta 152H.

**Ta 152H-0/H-2**

Considered by many *Luftwaffe* pilots to be the finest piston-engined fighter of the Second World War, the H-series was the only version of the Ta 152 to be put into service in significant numbers. It was powered by a Jumo 213E engine of 1,750 hp and had high aspect ratio wings of 47 ft 4 in span. The first fully equipped prototype was V-29/U1 (*Werke* Nr 0054) which

A former Fw 190C-1 prototype, V-30/U1 *Werke* Nr 0055 GH+KT became one of the prototypes for the Ta 152 and had its DB 603G replaced by a Jumo 213A. It was rebuilt with long-span wings and had its armament removed, but it crashed at Langenhagen on 13 August 1944. This view of V-30/U1 (below) emphasizes the long-span, high aspect ratio wings of the Ta 152. Also of note is the intake for the supercharger on the starboard side of the cowling (the intake for DB 603-powered aircraft was on the port side).

also had a pressurised cabin and an armament of one engine-mounted MK 108 and two MG 151/20 cannon in the wing roots. The pre-production H-0 was similar to V-29/U1 except that power could be boosted to 2,250 hp for short periods by MW-50 injection. The Ta 152H-1 was again similar to the H-0 but with increased fuel capacity of 130 gallons in the fuselage and a total of 88 gallons in the wings carried in five separate tanks. Further tanks were incorporated for MW-50 and GM-1.

**Final variants**

Final proposed variants in the series were the H-10, which would have been a photographic reconnaissance machine similar to the E-2, the two-seat S-1 fighter trainer and two projects based on the Ta 152, which would have been powered by a 2,500 hp Jumo 222E/F.

# Appendix 1
# Fw 190 Weapons and Systems

Throughout its life the Fw 190 carried a wide variety of weapons which, as the war progressed, were to be increased in number, weight and destructive firepower as targets became heavier and better protected. The following brief descriptions catalogue its main armament and the weapons it might have been required to carry had the war gone on any longer than it did.

## MACHINE-GUNS AND CANNON

**MG 17:** Developed by the Rheinmetall-Borsig company, the MG 17 was comparable to the American Browning 0.30-in and Russian ShKAS 7.62-mm machine-guns. It was the standard engine-mounted gun up to the Fw 190A-6 and was also fitted to the F-1/F-3. At 7.92 mm, it had a slightly higher calibre than its Allied contemporaries, and it was belt-fed. Its performance was sufficient to penetrate 5 mm thick armour plate at a distance of 100 metres, but strengthened rounds used later were capable of piercing 17 mm thick plate at a range of 50 metres. The use of self-sealing fuel tanks and heavier armour on bomber aircraft soon rendered the rifle calibre machine-gun obsolescent and attention quickly turned to the use of heavier guns of 13-, 20- and 30-mm calibre.

**MG 131:** Work on the 13-mm calibre MG 131 began at Rheinmetall-Borsig in 1933 and the first operational use of the weapon occurred in 1938. Equivalent to the 0.50-in Browning, the MG 131 fired a lighter round at a lower muzzle velocity (but at a slightly higher rate of fire) and was to be produced in a wide variety of versions. It was first used on the Fw 190A-5/U9, becoming standard armament on A-series aircraft from the A-7, and was also fitted to the Fw 190F-8 and F-9.

**MG FF:** A 20-mm cannon manufactured in Germany under licence from the Swiss Oerlikon company, the MG FF fired a 4.7-ounce round which was heavier than the French Hispano-Suiza and Russian ShVAK, but it had a lower rate of fire – only 350 rounds per minute – and lower muzzle velocity. Ammunition was contained in 45- or 60- round drums. The basic design of the weapon dated back to 1917 and owing to its relatively low hitting power it was replaced by the MG 151/20.

**MG 151/20:** Produced by Mauser, the MG 151/20 had a rate of fire of 750 rounds per minute and a muzzle velocity of 2,500 feet per second. Like the Russian ShVAK it fired a 3.5-ounce shell and was also

Close-up of the 30-mm MK 103 cannon as fitted to an Fw 190A-5/U11. The MK 103, developed by Rheinmetall-Borsig, fired an 11.6-ounce shell at a rate of 420 rounds per minute.

comparable in terms of weight and belt feed. Although it fired slightly faster than the 20-mm Hispano, its penetrative capability was considerably less owing to the latter's use of a heavier shell. The MG 151/20 appeared early in the Fw 190's development and was first used on the A-2 series, replacing the wing-root MG 17s.

**MK 103:** Another product of Rheinmetall-Borsig, the 30-mm MK 103 was first seen on the Fw 190A-5/U11. Although it fired a round of 11.6 ounces at a cyclic rate of 420 per minute, its accuracy was questionable and even after the introduction of a modified muzzle the spread of fire at close range was improved only by a small amount. Carriage of this weapon was usually in under-wing pods. This avoided the need for bulged fairings which would have been required for a wing-mounted installation because of the gun's dimensions.

**MK 108:** A much more advanced gun than the MK 103, the MK 108 was initially rejected by the Technical Office of the RLM and production did not commence until mid-1941. Its chief advantages were low weight (half that of the MK 103) and a high rate of fire, although the muzzle velocity was a modest 1,750 feet per second.

An Fw 190G-8 fitted with a Bv 246B *Hagelkorn* (Hailstone) glide bomb. The Bv 246B's cigar-shaped fuselage tapered to a cruciform tail, and had a shoulder-mounted high aspect ratio wing. Although 21 ft in span, its narrow chord meant that wing loading was 102 lb/sq ft. The bomb was guided by a gyroscope whose signals could be modified by a direction-finding device tuned to a radio beam from the parent aircraft. First produced in December 1943, the Bv 246B was not used operationally.

The SG 113 *Foerstersonde* weapon seen here installed in the wing of an Fw 190F-8. The SG 113 was designed as an anti-tank weapon and was of 77 mm calibre. Two guns were mounted in the lower half of each fairing, the upper fairings containing barrels in which counterweights were fired upwards to equalise the recoil forces. The guns were fired by a magnetic sensing device that was activated when the aircraft flew over its target at low level.

Even so, one hit from a high-explosive or incendiary shell was liable to destroy a twin-engined aircraft, and three or four hits were generally all that was needed to bring down a four-engined heavy bomber. First used on the Fw 190 A-5/U16, the under-wing installation required the fitting of a blast tube around the barrel to prevent damage due to the discharge of gas pressure as the gun was fired. Although a single hit could cause significant damage, the MK 108's low muzzle velocity meant that it took more than two seconds for each shell to travel 1,000 yards, during which time gravity drop was in the order of 100 ft. This meant that attacks had to be pressed home to relatively close range to ensure success.

**SG 113:** One of the most unusual weapons systems developed during the war, the SG 113 *Foerstersonde* was a 77-mm gun, two of which were carried vertically on each wing of an Fw 190F-8 between the fuselage and undercarriage unit. Intended as an anti-tank weapon, the

attacking aircraft flew at very low level and the gun was activated to fire vertically downwards by a magnetic detection device which was triggered as it flew over its victim. The gun barrels were housed in streamlined fairings and the recoil forces were countered by weights which were fired upwards in similar fairings mounted above the wing. Although tested successfully from late 1944, it appears not to have been used operationally.

**SG 116/117:** Working on a similar principle to the SG 113, the SG 116 *Zellendusche* was mounted vertically in the aft fuselage and comprised three, four or six MK 103 cannon which were intended to fire vertically at heavy bombers. The SG 117 *Rohrblock* employed seven MK 108 cannon bound together and testing was being carried out on Fw 190 V-74 (*Werke* Nr 733713) when the war came to an end.

## MISSILES

**WGr.21:** The WGr.21 was a 21-cm spin-stabilised rocket developed from a German army weapon. It weighed 248 lb, including a 90 lb warhead. The WGr.21 was carried in a simple tube launcher under each wing, and both rockets were launched together by a stick-mounted firing button. The weapon was time fused to detonate at a distance 600–1,200 yards after launch and was lethal to any target within 100 feet of the detonation point. The prime requirement was to inflict significant damage to heavy four-engined bombers from outside the range of their defensive fire, but in practice the rocket's relatively slow speed of 1,020 ft/sec made aiming difficult, a factor which was compounded by difficulty in assessing the range of the target.

Unsuccessful trials were also carried out with the 28-cm WGr.28/32 rocket which was carried either singly or in pairs under the wing of Fw 190F-8s.

**R4M 'Orkan':** Although used successfully by the Me 262s of JV 44, the R4M was only used experimentally on the Fw 190. Weighing a little over 7 lb it was 2 ft 8 in long with a diameter of 2 in and had folding fins which opened after firing to provide stability. Light enough to be carried in numbers – Me 262s were armed with twelve – one hit could bring down a bomber.

**R 100/BS:** A 21-cm incendiary rocket developed by Rheinmetall-Borsig, weighing 242 lb. It saw experimental use only.

**R 100/MS:** Identical to the R 100/BS but with an explosive warhead.

**RBS B/F21:** A 21-cm rocket bomb intended to be fired from an under-wing rail.

**X-4 'Ruhrstahl':** Powered by a BMW 109-548 rocket motor, the X-4 was an air-to-air missile that was to be fitted under-wing on ETC 503 racks and wire-guided to its target by the pilot of the launch aircraft. It was first flown from an Fw 190 on 11 August 1944 and although 1,000 missiles were produced by January 1945, destruction of the rocket motors at BMW's Stargard works led to the project being abandoned.

**Panzerblitz:** Three air-to-ground missiles carried this designation. The Panzerblitz 1 (Pb 1) was developed from a 78-mm rocket projectile used by the army and was used operationally in the last months of the war by Fw 190F-8/F-9s. A total of eight missiles could be carried (four under each wing) but as they could only be launched at low speeds, losses to ground fire were severe.

To get around this particular deficiency, the Panzerblitz 2 (Pb 2) was a development of the R4M missile that could penetrate 180 mm of armour. Up to fourteen missiles could be carried and this system was used against tanks on the Eastern Front by Fw 190F-9s from December 1944. The final Panzerblitz (Pb 3) was again based on the R4M. It featured a larger warhead but trials were not completed before the end of the war.

## BOMBS AND TORPEDOS

**BT 200/400/700/1000/1400/1850:** A range of Bomb-Torpedos were developed late in the war as it was hoped that they could be produced quicker and more cheaply than conventional torpedos. Weight ranged from 485 lb (220 lb charge) of the BT 200 to the 4,240 lb (2,315 lb charge) of the BT 1850. During trials difficulties were experienced with aiming and release, and although intended for use by Fw 190F-8s carrying ETC 502 racks, very few were used operationally.

**SC 50/250/500/1000/1800:** The Fw 190 was able to carry a wide range of SC or *Splitterbombe* (splinter bomb) types up to the SC 1800 weighing 3,968 lb including its explosive charge of 2,315 lb. The bombs most commonly used operationally were the SC 50 which weighed 110 lb with a 55 lb charge, the SC 250 of 551 lb (298 lb charge) and the SC 500 of 1,102 lb (595 lb

Fw 190A-5/U8 with an SC 500 bomb. The oval shape outboard of the undercarriage leg is the fixing for a Junkers-designed 66-gallon overload tank that featured a streamlined fairing. In practice simpler under-wing racks designed by Messerschmitt and Focke-Wulf proved to be superior, creating less drag.

Fw 190A-5/U14 with LTF 5b torpedo. Armament was limited to two wing root MG 151/20 cannon. TD+SI was demonstrated to *Luftwaffe* and German Navy personnel at Gotenschafen in August 1943, but no production examples were forthcoming.

charge). Fw 190s were also configured to carry the SB 1000 *Sprengbombe* (demolition bomb) and the AB 250 and 500 bomb containers which contained SD-2 bomblets.

**LTF 5b:** This air-launched torpedo had a length of 17 ft 7 in, weighed 1,686 lb and was flown on an Fw 190A-5/U14 (*Werke Nr 871*) modified with an extended tailwheel to provide the necessary ground clearance. Excessive drag meant that performance was below expectations. The combination was not proceeded with.

**Bv 246 *Hagelkorn*:** Produced by Blohm und Voss, the Bv 246 was an unpowered glide bomb featuring a cigar-shaped fuselage and high aspect ratio wings of 21 ft span. With a glide angle of 1:25, the Bv 246 could theoretically be launched 130 miles from its intended target at a height of 34,400 ft. Trials were carried out at Karlshagen in the latter half of 1944 with Fw 190A-4, F-8 and G-8 aircraft, as well as other types of carrier.

# Appendix 2
# Technical Specifications

### Focke-Wulf Fw 190A-8

**Dimensions:** Span 10.5 m (34 ft 5.37 in); Length 8.84 m (29 ft 0 in); Height 3.96 m (13 ft); Wing area 18.26 m² (196.5 sq ft)
**Weights:** Empty 3175 kg (7,000 lb); Loaded 4423 kg (9,750 lb); Maximum loaded 4901 kg (10,805 lb)
**Performance:** Maximum speed 656 km/h (408 mph) at 6000 m (19,686 ft); 571 km/h (355 mph) at sea level; Cruising speed 480 km/h (298 mph); Initial rate of climb 720 m (2,363 ft) per minute; Service ceiling 11400 m (37,403 ft)
**Range:** Normal on internal fuel 805 km (500 miles)
**Armament:** Two 13-mm MG 131 machine-guns over engine (400 rounds per gun); Two 20-mm MG 151/20 cannon in wing roots (250 rounds per gun); Two MG 151/20s in outer wing positions (125 rounds per gun) plus one SC 500 500-kg (1,102-lb) bomb. A 1000 kg/2,204-lb SB 1000 bomb could be carried if its fins were cropped
**Powerplant:** BMW 801D-2 air-cooled 14-cylinder two-row radial engine delivering 1268 kW (1,700 hp) at take-off, boosted to 1566 kW (2,100 hp) with MW-50 water-methanol injection)

### Focke-Wulf Fw 190D-9

**Dimensions:** Span 10.5 m (34 ft 5.37 in); Length 10.19 m (33 ft 5in); Height 3.36 m (11 ft); Wing Area 18.3 m² (196.98 sq ft)
**Weights:** Empty 3490 kg (7,694 lb); Loaded 4300 kg (9,480 lb); Maximum loaded 4840 kg (10,670 lb)
**Performance:** Maximum speed 685 km/h (426 mph) at 21,326 ft; 575 km/h (357 mph) at sea level (with MW-50); Climb to 10000 m (32,810 ft) in 16.8 min; Service ceiling 12000 m (39,370 ft)
**Range:** Normal (internal fuel) 840 km (520 miles)
**Armament:** Two 13-mm MG 131 machine-guns over engine (475 rounds per gun); Two 20-mm MG 151/20 cannon in wing roots (250 rounds per gun) plus one 500-kg (1,102-lb) SC 500 bomb
**Powerplant:** Junkers Jumo 213A 12-cylinder inverted-Vee, liquid-cooled in-line engine rated at 1324 kW (1,776 hp) at take-off, boosted to 1670 kW (2,240 hp) with MW-50 water-methanol injection.

# Appendix 3
# Fw 190 Production

Although Kurt Tank's main aim with the Fw 190 was to produce a fighter that could out-perform any other, his design philosophy was such that high levels of performance would not compromise ease of production and maintenance in the field. Production considerations were given high priority and this far-sighted policy was to be vindicated when the growing might of the Allied bomber offensive from 1942 made it imperative that facilities be widely dispersed.

The largest single component of the Fw 190 was the wing structure which was assembled as one unit, the single spar being continuous through the fuselage. The main spar was a built up 'I' section member of substantial construction in the centre-section, but with rapidly tapering top and bottom booms, while the web was a solid plate of the same thickness throughout its length. Bending moments were taken entirely by the main spar (near the centre-section) while

further out the spar flanges became of negligible size, bending being shared by the many L-section stringers. Throughout the wing, shear loads were taken by the main spar and the trailing edge member. This rear spar, which had a solid plate web, carried metal-framed fabric-covered ailerons and electrically operated all-metal split flaps. The wide-track undercarriage legs were hinged to the main spar and folded inwards into wells in the underside of the wing.

For a single-engined fighter that was likely to be subject to high load factors, wing ribs were relatively small in number and consisted of plate webs with their edges turned over to form flanges riveted to the skin. The rib flanges were cut away to clear the stringers and the ribs pierced with lightening holes with turned over edges for stiffening. The main spar and trailing edge member formed a torsion box with the top and bottom wing skin.

The stressed skin fuselage utilised twenty-one L-section stringers, with one wide top hat section stringer at the top, and L-section transverse formers about 18-in apart. It was built up from two main components, the forward section that extended from the firewall to the No. 8 bulkhead behind the pilot's seat, and the rear section which continued from this bulkhead to the jointing position for the tail assembly just forward of the fin. Two self-sealing fuel tanks were fitted in the lower part of the front fuselage, capable of holding 64 and 51 gallons respectively.

The wing was attached to the fuselage at five points, two vertical bolts passing through attachments at the top of the main spar, two horizontal pins at the roots of the light trailing edge member (which was not continuous) and one further horizontal pin joint at the centre of the main spar bottom boom. The latter connection was made to support the bottom spar boom laterally as the bottom central engine mounting tube was connected to the front side of the spar boom at that point. The BMW 801 air-cooled radial was carried on an engine mount with a total of five attachment points, two on the firewall and three on the main spar. Apart from the wing and the two main fuselage sections, the only other component of any great extent was the tail assembly with its integral fin, which featured a triangular door to allow access to the tailwheel retraction system and rudder cables. All other components were relatively small and were easily produced in engineering workshops widely scattered throughout Germany.

## Production

By the end of the war around 20,000 Fw 190s had been produced, although even this total is an approximate figure as many older airframes were subsequently rebuilt and re-appeared as newer variants. The main Focke-Wulf plants were at Bremen, Tutow/Mecklenburg, Marienburg, Cottbus, Sorau/Silesia, Neubrandenburg and Schwerin. From early 1942 production was expanded significantly and other manufacturers began to build the Fw 190 under licence including the Ago works at Oschersleben, Arado at

This underground production line of Fw 190A-8s was discovered after the war at Berlin's Tempelhof airport.

Babelsberg with subsidiary factories at Brandenburg, Warnemunde, Anklam, Rathenow, Wittenberge and Neuendorf, and Fieseler at Kassel. A production line was also set up at Cavant in France. After the war this plant produced the NC 900 (equivalent to the Fw 190A-5) that was used by the *Armée de l'Air* in the immediate post-war period. Other production facilities were discovered after the German collapse in May 1945, including an underground facility at Berlin's Tempelhof airport. Prior to its abandonment, component parts had been brought for assembly from all over Germany and finished examples of the Fw 190 had emerged onto the aerodrome for flight testing through a suitably shaped slot in a reinforced concrete wall at the end of the production line.

By early 1942 production of the Fw 190 was in excess of 250 per month although this figure could have been much higher. Proposed changes to the programme of aircraft production in 1941 were to have altered the build ratio of the Bf 109 to Fw 190 from four to one in the Messerschmitt's favour, to three to one against. Not surprisingly this greatly alarmed everyone on the Messerschmitt staff at Augsberg and in the discussions that took place afterwards they were to argue that the changeover would have an adverse effect on fighter production for many months as factories geared up to produce the Fw 190. As Germany had recently invaded Russia and was faced with ever-increasing aircraft production by the USA and the UK, this was a significant factor. Messerschmitt were also able to prove that Ernst Udet's Air Armament department had supplied false documentation that favoured the Focke-Wulf fighter. As a result many of the provisions of the revised production plan were scrapped and the Bf 109 was to be produced in far larger numbers for the remainder of the war. By the end of the conflict somewhere around 35,000 Bf 109s had been built, a figure almost double that for the superior Fw 190.

# Appendix 4
# Museum Aircraft and Survivors

**Fw 190A-2 *Werke Nr 5476 (N6152P)* – JG 5:** Owned by Wade S. Haynes and located at Anson, Texas.

**Fw 190A-3 – *Werke Nr 2219* – 14./JG 5:** In storage Bodo/Gardemoen prior to rebuild for Norwegian Air Force Museum.

**Fw 190A-5 – *Werke Nr 1227 (N19027)* – 4./JG 54:** Owned by Flying Heritage Collection of Seattle and currently on rebuild in the UK.

**Fw 190A-6 – *Werke Nr 550214:*** On display at the South African National Museum of Military History, Saxonwold coded PN+LU. Built by Ago at Oschersleben in mid-1943, 550214 is thought to have flown with III./NJG 11, a night-fighter unit. Its cockpit shows it to have been equipped with FuG 217 *Neptun* radar. It came into RAF control at Leck and was flown from Schleswig to Farnborough on 16 June 1945. It was subsequently shown at a display of captured aircraft in Hyde Park, London before being shipped to South Africa in October 1946.

**Fw 190A-6 – *Werke Nr 550470 (N126JG)* – I./JG 26:** One of two Fw 190s owned by Malcolm Laing. Based at Lubbock, Texas.

**Fw 190A-8 – *Werke Nr '170393'* – 6./JG 1:** Replica with some original parts for the *Luftfahrtmuseum*, Hanover.

**Fw 190A-8 – *Werke Nr 173056 (N91169):*** Second of two Fw 190s owned by Malcom Laing and based at Chandler, Arizona. Being restored.

**Fw 190A-8 – *Werke Nr 173889* – 7./JG 1:** Under restoration for Dr Mark Timken.

**Fw 190A-8 – *Werke Nr 350177 (N4247L)* – 12./JG 5:** Owned by John W. Houston, Texas Air Museum, Rio Hondo, Texas.

**Fw 190A-8 – *Werke Nr 730924:*** NC 900 preserved at the Musée de l'Air in Paris.

**Fw 190A-8 – *Werke Nr 732070* – 12./JG 5:** Under restoration for Texas Air Museum.

**Fw 190A-8 – *Werke Nr 732183 (N90FW)* – 12./JG 5:** Owned by John W. Houston and under restoration at the Texas Air Museum. Crashed near Herdla in Norway on 9 February 1945 after attacking a Beaufighter of 144 Squadron, probably shot down by a Mustang of 65 Squadron. The pilot, *Leutnant* Rudi Linz, was killed. At the time of his death Linz had 79 victories to his credit, most of these having been achieved in Russia.

**Fw 190A-8 – *Werke Nr 733682:*** Top half of *Mistel* S-3B composite (Ju 88H-4). On display at the Imperial War Museum in London.

**Fw 190D-9 – *Werke Nr 210968* – 2./JG 26:** Recovered from Lake Schwerin and under restoration for the *Luftwaffe* Museum, Berlin/Gatow.

**Fw 190D-9 – *Werke Nr 601088:*** Built by Fieseler at Kassel, ex-IV(*Sturm*)./JG 3 and FE-120. Currently with the USAF Museum Wright-Patterson AFB, Dayton, Ohio, on loan from the National Air and Space Museum.

**Fw 190D-13 – *Werke Nr 836017 (N190D):*** Ex-Yellow 10 of I./JG 26. Flown by *Oberstleutnant* Heinz Lange in mock combat with Hawker Tempest after the war. Evaluated in USA as FE-118 and then donated to Georgia Technical University after evaluation; then went through several changes of ownership until 1972 when a restoration was carried out by Williams Flugzeuge in Germany under a contract from the Champlin Fighter Museum, Mesa, Arizona. Still at Champlin and potentially airworthy.

**Fw 190F-3 – *Werke Nr 670071* – 1./SchG 1:** Under restoration for the Flugplatz Museum, Cottbus.

**Fw 190F-8 – *Werke Nr 5415:*** Status uncertain, reported to have been under restoration for the Old Flying Machine Company in New Zealand.

**Fw 190F-8 – *Werke Nr 930838:*** Part of the Yugoslav Aeronautical Museum in Belgrade, currently stored.

**Fw 190F-8 – *Werke Nr 931862 (N91FW):*** On 9 February 1945 Beaufighters of the Dallachy Strike Wing escorted by P-51 Mustangs of 65 Squadron attacked a German convoy in Fordefjord, Norway. Nine Fw 190F-8s of 9./JG 5 were scrambled from Herdla to intercept, including 931862 flown by *Unteroffizier* Heinz Orlowski. During a dogfight with a P-51, Orlowski's aircraft was hit and he baled out at a height of only 300 ft. His parachute did not have time to open but luck was with him as he fell into a deep snow bank and survived, his aircraft crashing onto a remote hillside. It remained there until 1983 when the remains were recovered and eventually passed to the Kongelige Norsk Luftforssvaret collection in Bergen. A restoration to static condition by John W. Houston of the Texas Air Museum took place in 1992 and the aircraft is currently at Kissimmee, Florida for restoration to airworthy status. Owned by Dr Mark Timken.

**Fw 190F-8 – *Werke* Nr 931884:** Built by Arado at Warnemünde as an A-4 (*Werke* Nr 640069), a rebuild to F-8 standard was undertaken by Fieseler and the revised *Werke* Nr 931884 allotted. The aircraft then saw service with I./SG 2 on the Eastern Front until capture by US forces. It was then shipped to the USA for evaluation and marked as FE-117. Following a period of storage it was acquired by the National Air and Space Museum and was restored in the early 1980s. Currently part of the NASM's Paul E. Garber facility.

**Fw 190F-8/U1 – *Werke* Nr 584219:** The only two-seat Fw 190 in existence, 584219 was used by *Jagdfliegerschule* 103 as a VIP transport and was captured at Grove in Norway and flown to Farnborough via Gilze-Rijen on 2 September 1945. It was given Air Ministry No. 29. After evaluation by the RAE it was flown to 6 MU at Brize Norton before moving on to 76 MU Wroughton. It was then stored at various locations including Stanmore Park, Fulbeck, Gaydon and Henlow before becoming a popular exhibit at the Historic Aircraft Museum at St Athan. It is now on display in the Bomber Command Hall of the RAF Museum at Hendon.

**Ta 152H-0:** – Preserved at the NASM, Washington DC. Various *Werke* numbers have been quoted for the only remaining Ta 152. Initially thought to have been 150003, other sources maintain that it is 150010,

Fw 190A-8 *Werke* Nr 733682 on display at the Imperial War Museum in London. Formerly the upper half of a *Mistel* combination, mounted above a Junkers Ju 88H-4 bomber.

although restoration work carried out in late 1998 resulted in a third possibility, 150020. Formerly Green 4 of JG 301, it was recovered by the British in Aalborg and tested at Wright Field, Ohio as FE-112 (later T2-112). Stored until 1960, it was then presented to NASM. Currently part of the Paul Garber facility.

**New production:** In 1996 it was announced that a new German company, Flug Werk GmbH, was about to embark on a limited production run of twelve Fw 190A-8/N aircraft, the N standing for *Nachbau* or remake. Original manufacturers drawings have been used wherever possible but where these have not been available, original parts have been used as patterns. The manufacturers claim the airframe to be 98% true to the original and all twelve aircraft have original tailwheel units. The aircraft will be fitted with a Russian-built 14-cylinder ASh 82 radial of 1,900 hp with direct fuel injection, giving a maximum speed of 395 mph at 20,000 ft, a cruising speed of 365 mph at 2,300 rpm and an initial climb rate of 4,000 ft/min. At the time of writing the first machine was close to its maiden flight.

# Appendix 5
# Fw 190 Models, Decals and Parts

| Maker/Variant | Year | Ref | Remarks |
|---|---|---|---|
| **Academy** | | | |
| Fw 190A-8 | 1994 | 178 | Kit also used as base for MPM model of Fw 190A-5/U14 torpedo fighter (MPM ref 72048) |
| Fw 190D-9 | 1998 | 1660 | Bulged hood. Decals for IV./JG 3 aircraft of *Oblt* Oscar Romm |
| **Airfix** | | | |
| Fw 190D-9 | 1955 | 1064 | Standard hood. Revised and reissued in 1976. Decals for aircraft of IV./JG 3 (Romm) and 6./ JG 26 Nordhorn, March 1945 |
| Fw 190F-8 | 1977 | 2063 | First Airfix kit of BMW 801-powered aircraft |
| Fw 190A-8 | 1982 | 4001 | Revised kit giving option of A-8/F-8 and offering various armament combinations. Decals for aircraft of II./JG 1, *Major* Heinz Bar |
| **Aoshima** | | | |
| Ta 152H-0 | 1997 | 16503 | Decals for various *Stab*/JG 300 aircraft. Revision of this kit as Ta 152H-1 issued by Aoshima (1997) |
| **Dragon DHL** | | | |
| Ta 152 H-1 | 1992 | 5008 | Chinese kit, not for beginners. Can be built with open cowling to show detailed engine. Decals for aircraft of JG 301 |
| Ta 152C-0 | 1997 | 5007-1 | Similar to above but without engine detail and with short-span wings of C-0. Aircraft portrayed is V7 CI+XM *Werke* Nr 110007 |
| **Hasegawa** | | | |
| Fw 190A-5 | 1970 | | Original kit revised many times, commencing in 1985/86 with versions for the A-8 and F-8, plus the A-8/R11 night-fighter. Most recent issues are for G-8 (1999) with flame dampers and LR tanks and A-6 (2001) |
| Fw 190D-9 | 1970 | | Original kit revised in 1992 (ref AP6). Decals for Fw Werner Hohenberg (4./JG 2), *Oblt* Oscar Romm (I./JG 3) *Major* Gerhard Barkhorn (JG 6) and *Hptm* Waldemar Wubke (JV 44). Reissued again in 1995 as aircraft of JV 44 *Platzschutzstaffel* with red undersides and white stripes |
| **Heller** | | | |
| Fw 190A-5 | 1963 | L087 | Could be built to represent aircraft up to the A-8. Basic kit revised in the 1970s to include an F-series aircraft with decals for an A-8/R2 of IV(*Sturm*)./JG 3 or an F-8 of an unknown unit |
| **Italeri** | | | |
| Fw 190D-9 | 1978 | 128 | Reasonable quality, could be built with canopy in open position |
| Fw 190A-8 | 1995 | 178 | Decals for A-8 of II./JG 300 or F-8 of unknown unit |
| **Matchbox** | | | |
| Fw 190A-3 | 1972 | PK-6 | Kit originally representing the Fw 190A-3/A-4, reissued later with decals for an A-4 'Red 10' of III./JG 51 and a G-3 of SG 1 |
| **Monogram** | | | |
| Fw 190A-8 | 1997 | 5943 | Pro-Modeler series. Can be built to represent the A-8, F-8 or G-8. Decals for A-8 of 3./JG 54, A-8 of Fw Bindsell, 6./JG 1 or A-8/R11 night-fighter of Fw Migge, I./NJGr 10 |
| **Revell** | | | |
| Fw 190A-8 | 1997 | 4118 | Revision of Monogram Pro-Modeler A-8 kit. Can be converted into A-8/R11 night-fighter or built as an F-8 |
| Fw 190A-8 | 1999 | 4169 | As above but featuring the Bv 246 Hagelkorn glide bomb |
| Fw 190F-8 | 2000 | 4147 | As above but revised as F-8/R14 torpedo fighter. Decals for aircraft of II./KG 200 Flensburg April 1945 or *Erprobungsstaffel* 1944 |
| **Sword** | | | |
| Fw 190A-1 | 2000 | 72008 | Decals for A-1 of *Oblt* Walter Schneider of II./JG 26. Variable position flaps |
| **Tamiya** | | | |
| Fw 190D-9 | 2000 | 60751 | Features bulged hood and has decals for aircraft of 4./JG 301 Straubing, and *Stab*/JG 4 Rhein-Main, both early 1945 |
| Fw 190A-3 | 2001 | 60766 | Generally regarded as the best early A-series model, decals are provided for aircraft of 8./JG 2, III./JG 2 (*Hptm* Hans 'Assi' Hahn) and *Stab*/JG 26 (*Hptm* Wilhelm Gath) |

# Appendix 6
# Fw 190 Books

**Campbell, Jerry L:** Focke-Wulf 190 in Action
*Squadron/Signal, 1975*

**Ethell, Jeffrey L:** Monogram Close Up 24 – Ta 152
*Monogram Aviation Publications, 1990*

**Filley, Brian:** Fw 190A, F and G in Action
*Squadron/Signal, 1999*

**Jessen, Morten:** Focke-Wulf 190 – The Birth of the Butcher Bird 1939–43
*Greenhill Books,1998*

**Laing, Malcolm and Ryle E.Brown:** Fw 190A/F Walk Around
*Squadron/Signal, 2000*

**Mombeek, Eric, with Forsyth, Robert and Creek, Eddie J:** Sturmstaffel 1
*Classic Publications, 1999*

**Nowarra, Heinz J:** The Focke-Wulf 190 – A Famous German Fighter
*Harleyford, 1965*

**Nowarra, Heinz J:** Focke-Wulf Fw 190 – Ta 152
*Motorbuch, 1987*

**Price, Alfred:** Focke-Wulf 190 At War
*Ian Allan, 1977*

**Price, Alfred:** Focke-Wulf Fw 190 in Combat
*Sutton Publishing, 1998*

**Smith, J. and Creek, E:** Fw 190D
*Monogram, 1986*

**Swanborough, Gordon and Green, William:** The Focke-Wulf Fw 190
*David and Charles, 1976*

**Trojca, Waldemar:** Focke-Wulf Fw 190
*Model Hobby, 2001*

**Weal, John:** Focke-Wulf Fw 190 Aces of the Eastern Front
*Osprey, 1995*

**Weal, John:** Focke-Wulf Fw 190 Aces of the Western Front
*Osprey, 1996*

# Index